29.95
80E

GREEK VERB ENDINGS:
a Reverse Index
(revised and expanded)

Thomas A. Robinson

The Edwin Mellen Press
Lewiston/ Queenston/ Lampeter
1989

Greek Verb Endings: A Reverse Index
by Thomas A. Robinson

ISBN 0-88946-206-2

For information, contact:

The Edwin Mellen Press
Box 450
Lewiston, New York
USA 14092

The Edwin Mellen Press
Box 67
Queenston, Ontario
L0S 1L0 CANADA

The Edwin Mellen Press, Ltd.
Lampeter, Dyfed, Wales
United Kingdom   SA48 7DY

Printed in the United States of America

to my Mother,
MARY A. ROBINSON,
for her many sacrifices

A NOTE ABOUT ERRORS AND OMISSIONS:
In a work of this nature, errors and omissions will have occurred. The users of this index will provide an invaluable service by bringing these to the attention of the author.

Preface

Including the participle forms, it is possible for a Greek verb to have over 700 different endings! Not surprising then that it is the Greek verb that stumps most readers of Greek.

Greek Verb Endings: a Reverse Index is an attempt to make the host of Greek verb forms readily available to even the beginning student of Greek. The project was started over ten years ago, just after I had completed my undergraduate studies in Greek. Initially my aim was to reorganize the paradigms so that I would not need to search endlessly for some unfamiliar form. Several different arrangements were tried, and countless hours of compiling and revising and compiling again became my 'hobby' during my graduate studies. The paradigms in my Greek grammars became almost illegible as I marked off each verb ending when I inserted it into some new arrangement.

I finally arrived at a scheme that makes it possible for the reader of Hellenistic and Classical Greek to identify almost any verb or participle ending (from the most common to the most obscure) in as little time as it takes to look up an English word in *Webster's*. The reverse alphabetical order of the lists provides the key to the simplicity that a work of this nature requires if it is to be a tool of ready use. (See 'Instructions' for more details.)

Several other aids have been provided. Each is intended to eliminate that familiar (but not fond) activity of all readers of Greek—the searching of endless paradigms for a forgotten (or never-learned) ending or for an unknown irregular root.

Does all this remove my work from the camp of the language 'purists'? Is my work just another language 'crutch,' making Greek easier than what it really 'should' be?

I hope so.

Thomas A. Robinson

Contents

Forms Not Included

- SOME LABIAL AND GUTTURAL FORMS:
  Some Labial and Guttural forms differ from the regular form only in that σ of the regular form is modified to ψ for the labials and to ξ for the gutturals. To find such labial or guttural endings in the lists, replace ψ or ξ with the regular tense formant σ.

- UNCONTRACTED VOWEL CONTRACT FORMS:
  Frequently an author will use uncontracted endings for verbs that normally are contracted. These uncontracted endings are simply the regular endings attached directly to the vowel of the vowel contract verbs. They can, therefore, be found in the main lists under the ★ entry.

- FUTURES OF VOWEL CONTRACT VERBS
  AND UNTHEMATIC VERBS:
  Futures of vowel contract verbs and unthematic verbs merely lengthen the final stem vowel. As for the endings, no unusual change occurs, therefore such endings can be found easily in the main lists.

- οω CONTRACT VERBS:
  Some οω verbs have ω and ῳ instead of ου and οι. Simply replace ω with ου and ῳ with οι to find these endings in the main lists.

- Two MI verbs are exceptions. Καθημαι has η where one would expect α, and κειμαι has ει where one would expect ε. Simply replace η with α and ει with ε to find these endings in the main lists.

- VOCATIVE FORMS OF PARTICIPLES:These forms are identical to the nominative forms.

Abbreviations

Acc	Accusative
C	Consonant Stem
D	Dental
Fem	Feminine
G	Guttural
I •	Infinitive
L	Labial
LG	Liquid (and Nasal)
Masc	Masculine
MI	μι stems
Mid	Middle
N	Noun, Pronoun or Adjective
Nom	Nominative
P •	Participle
Pass	Passive Voice
V •	Verb
V	Vowel Contract Stem

Instructions

This **reverse** index of GREEK VERB ENDINGS makes it possible to identify any verb or participle ending (from the most common to the most obscure) in no more time than it takes to look up an English word in *Webster's*. It differs from the alphabetical format of a standard dictionary or lexicon in that the endings are grouped in terms of a common final letter rather than in terms of a common first letter. This arrangement is the key to the simplicity that a work of this nature requires if it is to be a tool of ready use, enabling the user to identify the verb ending even when the reader is unable to distinguish the stem from the ending. **Note: Hellenistic and Attic forms are found in the main lists; dialectic variations are found in an appendix.**

TO FIND A PARTICULAR ENDING IN THE LISTS:
* If the reader can identify the part of the verb that forms the ending, simply work from the last letter of the ending towards the first, keeping in mind the reverse alphabetical format of the lists.
* If the reader cannot identify the part of the verb that forms the ending, simply work from the last letter of the verb towards the first letter of the verb until the longest entry in the lists is reached. Except in a few cases, that entry will indicate the ending of the verb in question.

TO ILLUSTRATE **REVERSE** ALPHABETICAL ORDER:
First with an example from English. Suppose one were to look for the word **study**. One first looks under **y**. There will be found all the words that end with the letter **y.** Then one looks for the letter **d**, finding there all the words that end with **dy**. And then the letter **u (udy)**, then **t (tudy)**, and finally **s (study)**.

In the same way, Greek endings can be found in this index. Consider the Greek ending ομεν: first look under the letter ν. There will be found all the verb endings that end with the letter ν. Then look for the letter ε. There will be found all endings ending with the letters εν. Then the letter μ to find all endings ending with the letters μεν. Finally look for the letter ο. There the user will find the complete verb ending ομεν, followed by all possible meanings of that ending.

SAMPLE ENDING:
Each one-line entry has three parts, marked off by black dots.

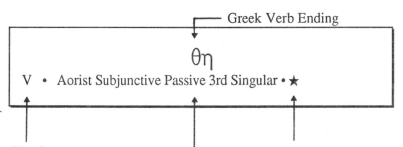

The first element of
each line is one of the
following four letters:

V - finite verb ending
I - infinitive ending
P - participle ending
N - noun/adjective ending

The third element is a list
of all classes of verbs for
which that entry is
applicable. Abbreviations
and codes are used here
and are explained more
fully at the beginning of the
index. (Only when more
than one entry is given is it
necessary to consult the
third part of the entry.)

The second element is the full parsing
of the verb ending.
• For finite endings:
tense, mood, voice, person, and number
• For infinitive endings:
tense and voice
• For participle endings:
tense, voice, case, gender, and number
• For noun/adjective endings:
declension, case, number, and gender

Explanation of Codes

THE REGULAR VERB: Verbs with roots ending in υ or ι do not contract vowels or modify consonants. Such verbs are considered the regular verbs for verb paradigms. All other verbs depart from the scheme of the regular verb in some of the forms, but never in all forms. Non-regular verbs will contract vowels and modify consonants only if two vowels or two consonants come together when the ending is added to the stem. This is expressed simply on the chart below, where V = Vowel and C = Consonant.

DIFFERENT FROM ★ FORMS:
Stem / C + C / ending
Stem / V + V / ending
IDENTICAL TO ★ FORMS:
Stem / C + V / ending
Stem / V + C / ending

In this index, ★ indicates:
- the form of the regular verb
- the form of the vowel contract stems if the ending begins with a consonant
- the form of the consonant stems if the ending begins with a vowel
- the form of μι verbs except for the present, imperfect, and second aorist.
- [Note: Sometimes an author will use a ★ form when a different form would more widely be used with that particular verb. If no entry can be found for a particular ending of verbs from a specific class, try the entry for the ★ form.

1

STRONG OR SECOND TENSES: These verbs omit the tense
formant usually found in the perfect active, the future passive,
and the aorist of all voices. (In the case of the strong aorist
active and middle, secondary personal endings are used.)

2

ROOT AORISTS: These verbs use the personal endings of the μι
verb, and like the strong tenses, omit the tense formant. The
following words follow these forms: ἔβην (βαινω), ἔφθην
(φθανω), ἔδραν (διδρασκω), ἔγνων (γιγνωσκω), ἑαλων
(ἁλισκομαι), ἐβιων (ζαω), ἔδυν (δυομαι), and ἔφυν (φυομαι).

3

AFFECTED TENSE FORMANT: Many verbs use the thematic
personal endings, but in some way modify (or omit) the tense
formant. The most common verb in this group is the Liquid.
The loss of a tense formant frequently requires a contraction of
vowels.
FUTURE (often called 'Contract Future'):
• Liquids and Nasals
• Attic futures
• Doric futures (tense formant is retained; contraction of
vowels nonetheless occurs)
AORIST:
• Liquids and Nasals
• κ – Aorist [These verbs (all MI) differ from the first
aorists only in that that standard tense formant of the
aorists (σ) is replaced by κ.]

4

A few common αω contract verbs present unusual vowel contraction in the present forms of the indicative, the subjuctive, and the imperative, and in the imperfect. The following words follow these forms: διψω, ζω, πεινω, κνω, νω, σμω, χρω, χρωμαι, and ψω.

5

Some common words have retained more primitive endings, in particular εἰμι and φημι.

The following two symbols (▲ and *) are placed before the Greek verb ending.

The process of the intrusion of weak aorist forms into the strong aorist and of strong aorist forms into the weak aorist has reached a stage in Modern Greek where there is only one set of endings for weak and strong aorist and the imperfect:
α, ες, ε, αμεν, ατε, ετε, αν.
The user of this index should be aware of the possibility of such variation for any ending marked ▲.

The symbol * is used to indicate the presence of a liquid or a nasal consonant in this position.

α

▲ α

V • Present Imperative Active 2nd Singular • αω
V • Imperfect Indicative Active 3rd Singular • αω
V • Aorist Indicative Active 1st Singular • 3
V • 2nd Aorist Indicative Active 3rd Singular • 2
V • 2nd Aorist Imperative Active 2nd Singular • αμι
V • 2nd Perfect Indicative Active 1st Singular • 1
N • See Case Ending List

ą

V • Present Indicative Active 3rd Singular • αω
V • Present Indicative Middle/Passive 2nd Singular • αω
V • Present Subjunctive Active 3rd Singular • αω
V • Present Subjunctive Middle/Passive 2nd Singular • αω
V • 2nd Aorist Subjunctive Active 3rd Singular • 2
N • See Case Ending List

μεθα

V • Perfect Indicative Middle/Passive 1st Plural • ★ C
V • Pluperfect Indicative Middle/Passive 1st Plural • ★ C

αμεθα

V • Present Indicative Middle/Passive 1st Plural • αμι
V • Imperfect Indicative Middle/Passive 1st Plural • αμι
V • 2nd Aorist Indicative Middle 1st Plural • αμι
V • Aorist Indicative Middle 1st Plural • 3

σαμεθα

V • Aorist Indicative Middle 1st Plural • ★

εμεθα

V • Present Indicative Middle/Passive 1st Plural • εμι
V • Imperfect Indicative Middle/Passive 1st Plural • εμι
V • 2nd Aorist Indicative Middle 1st Plural • εμι

αιμεθα

V • Present Optative Middle/Passive 1st Plural • αμι
V • 2nd Aorist Optative Middle 1st Plural • αμι
V • Aorist Optative Middle 1st Plural • 3

σαιμεθα

V • Aorist Optative Middle 1st Plural • ★

ειμεθα

V • Present Optative Middle/Passive 1st Plural • εμι
V • 2nd Aorist Optative Middle 1st Plural • εμι

οιμεθα

V • Present Optative Middle/Passive 1st Plural • ★ εω οω ομι υμι
V • Future Optative Middle 1st Plural • 3
V • 2nd Aorist Optative Middle 1st Plural • ομι 1

σοιμεθα

V • Future Optative Middle 1st Plural • ★
V • Future Perfect Optative Passive 1st Plural • ★

(θ)ησοιμεθα

V • (1st) 2nd Future Optative Passive 1st Plural • ★ 1

ομεθα

V • Present Indicative Middle/Passive 1st Plural • ★ ομι
V • Imperfect Indicative Middle/Passive 1st Plural • ★ ομι
V • 2nd Aorist Indicative Middle 1st Plural • ομι 1

σομεθα

V • Future Indicative Middle 1st Plural • ★
V • Future Perfect Indicative Passive 1st Plural • ★

(θ)ησομεθα

V • (1st) 2nd Future Indicative Passive 1st Plural • ★ 1

υμεθα

V • Present Indicative Middle/Passive 1st Plural • υμι
V • Imperfect Indicative Middle/Passive 1st Plural • υμι

ουμεθα

V • Present Indicative Middle/Passive 1st Plural • εω οω
V • Imperfect Indicative Middle/Passive 1st Plural • εω οω
V • Future Indicative Middle 1st Plural • 3

ωμεθα

V • Present Subjunctive Middle/Passive 1st Plural • ★ V MI 4
V • Present Indicative Middle/Passive 1st Plural • αω 4
V • Imperfect Indicative Middle/Passive 1st Plural • αω 4
V • Aorist Subjunctive Middle 1st Plural • 3
V • 2nd Aorist Subjunctive Middle 1st Plural • 1 αμι εμι ομι

ῳμεθα

V • Present Optative Middle/Passive 1st Plural • αω

σωμεθα

V • Aorist Subjunctive Middle 1st Plural • ★

σθα

V • Imperfect Indicative Active 2nd Singular • 5

(κ)υια

V • See Periphrastic Chart
P • (1st) 2nd Perfect Active Nominative Feminine Singular • ★ 1

(κ)υιᾳ

P • (1st) 2nd Perfect Active Dative Feminine Singular • ★ 1

κα

V • Perfect Indicative Active 1st Singular • ★
V • Aorist Indicative Active 1st Singular • 3 MI

μενα

V • See Periphrastic Chart
P • See Participle Chart A

σα

V • Aorist Indicative Active 1st Singular • ★
P • See Participle Chart B

ντα

P • See Participle Chart C

(κ)οτα

V • See Periphrastic Chart
P • (1st) 2nd Perfect Active Nominative/Accusative Neuter Plural • ★ 1
P • (1st) 2nd Perfect Active Accusative Masculine Singular • ★ 1

ε

▲ ε

V • Present Imperative Active 2nd Singular • ★
V • Imperfect Indicative Active 3rd Singular • ★
V • Aorist Indicative Active 3rd Singular • 3
V • 2nd Aorist Indicative Active 3rd Singular • 1
V • 2nd Aorist Imperative Active 2nd Singular • 1
V • 2nd Perfect Indicative Active 3rd Singular • 1
V • 2nd Perfect Imperative Active 2nd Singular • 1
N • See Case Ending List

*θε

V • Perfect Indicative Middle/Passive 2nd Plural • LQ
V • Perfect Imperative Middle/Passive 2nd Plural • LQ
V • Pluperfect Indicative Middle/Passive 2nd Plural • LQ

σθε

V • Perfect Indicative Middle/Passive 2nd Plural • ★ D
V • Perfect Imperative Middle/Passive 2nd Plural • ★ D
V • Pluperfect Indicative Middle/Passive 2nd Plural • ★ D

ασθε

V • Present Indicative Middle/Passive 2nd Plural • αω αμι 4
V • Present Subjunctive Middle/Passive 2nd Plural • αω
V • Present Imperative Middle/Passive 2nd Plural • αω αμι 4
V • Imperfect Indicative Middle/Passive 2nd Plural • αω αμι 4
V • Aorist Indicative Middle 2nd Plural • 3
V • Aorist Imperative Middle 2nd Plural • 3
V • 2nd Aorist Indicative Middle 2nd Plural • αμι
V • 2nd Aorist Imperative Middle 2nd Plural • αμι

σασθε

V • Aorist Indicative Middle 2nd Plural • ★
V • Aorist Imperative Middle 2nd Plural • ★

εσθε

V • Present Indicative Middle/Passive 2nd Plural • ★ εμι
V • Present Imperative Middle/Passive 2nd Plural • ★ εμι
V • Imperfect Indicative Middle/Passive 2nd Plural • ★ εμι
V • 2nd Aorist Indicative Middle 2nd Plural • εμι 1
V • 2nd Aorist Imperative Middle 2nd Plural • εμι 1

σεσθε

V • Future Indicative Middle 2nd Plural • ★
V • Future Perfect Indicative Passive 2nd Plural • ★

(θ)ησεσθε

V • (1st) 2nd Future Indicative Passive 2nd Plural • ★ 1

ησθε

V • Present Subjunctive Middle/Passive 2nd Plural • ★ εω αμι εμι υμι 4
V • 2nd Aorist Subjunctive Middle 2nd Plural • 1 αμι εμι
V • Present Indicative Middle/Passive 2nd Plural • 4
V • Present Imperative Middle/Passive 2nd Plural • 4
V • Imperfect Indicative Middle/Passive 2nd Plural • 4
V • Aorist Subjunctive Middle 2nd Plural • 3

σησθε

V • Aorist Subjunctive Middle 2nd Plural • ★

αισθε

V • Present Optative Middle/Passive 2nd Plural • αμι
V • 2nd Aorist Optative Middle 2nd Plural • αμι
V • Aorist Optative Middle 2nd Plural • 3

σαισθε

V • Aorist Optative Middle 2nd Plural • ★

εισθε

V • Present Indicative Middle/Passive 2nd Plural • εω
V • Present Imperative Middle/Passive 2nd Plural • εω
V • Imperfect Indicative Middle/Passive 2nd Plural • εω
V • Present Optative Middle/Passive 2nd Plural • εμι
V • 2nd Aorist Optative Middle 2nd Plural • εμι
V • Future Indicative Middle 2nd Plural • 3

οισθε

V • Present Optative Middle/Passive 2nd Plural • ★ εω οω ομι υμι
V • 2nd Aorist Optative Middle 2nd Plural • ομι 1
V • Future Optative Middle 2nd Plural • 3

σοισθε

V • Future Optative Middle 2nd Plural • ★
V • Future Perfect Optative Passive 2nd Plural • ★

(θ)ησοισθε

V • (1st) 2nd Future Optative Passive 2nd Plural • ★ 1

οσθε

V • Present Indicative Middle/Passive 2nd Plural • ομι
V • Present Imperative Middle/Passive 2nd Plural • ομι
V • Imperfect Indicative Middle/Passive 2nd Plural • ομι
V • 2nd Aorist Indicative Middle 2nd Plural • ομι
V • 2nd Aorist Imperative Middle 2nd Plural • ομι

υσθε

V • Present Indicative Middle/Passive 2nd Plural • υμι
V • Present Imperative Middle/Passive 2nd Plural • υμι
V • Imperfect Indicative Middle/Passive 2nd Plural • υμι

ουσθε

V • Present Indicative Middle/Passive 2nd Plural • οω
V • Present Imperative Middle/Passive 2nd Plural • οω
V • Imperfect Indicative Middle/Passive 2nd Plural • οω

ωσθε

V • Present Subjunctive Middle/Passive 2nd Plural • οω ομι
V • 2nd Aorist Subjunctive Middle 2nd Plural • ομι

ῳσθε

V • Present Optative Middle/Passive 2nd Plural • αω

φθε

V • Perfect Indicative Middle/Passive 2nd Plural • L
V • Perfect Imperative Middle/Passive 2nd Plural • L
V • Pluperfect Indicative Middle/Passive 2nd Plural • L

χθε

V • Perfect Indicative Middle/Passive 2nd Plural • G
V • Perfect Imperative Middle/Passive 2nd Plural • G
V • Pluperfect Indicative Middle/Passive 2nd Plural • G

ειε

V • Aorist Optative Active 3rd Singular • 3

σειε

V • Aorist Optative Active 3rd Singular • ★

κε

V • Perfect Indicative Active 3rd Singular • ★
V • Perfect Imperative Active 2nd Singular • ★
V • Aorist Indicative Active 3rd Singular • 3 MI

σε

V • Aorist Indicative Active 3rd Singular • ★

τε

V • 2nd Perfect Indicative Active 2nd Plural • MI
V • 2nd Perfect Imperative Active 2nd Plural • MI
V • 2nd Pluperfect Indicative Active 2nd Plural • MI

▲ ατε

V • Present Indicative Active 2nd Plural • αω αμι
V • Present Subjunctive Active 2nd Plural • αω
V • Present Imperative Active 2nd Plural • αω αμι
V • Imperfect Indicative Active 2nd Plural • αω αμι
V • Aorist Indicative Active 2nd Plural • 3
V • Aorist Imperative Active 2nd Plural • 3
V • 2nd Aorist Indicative Active 2nd Plural • 2
V • 2nd Aorist Subjunctive Active 2nd Plural • 2
V • 2nd Aorist Imperative Active 2nd Plural • 2
V • 2nd Perfect Indicative Active 2nd Plural • 1

κατε

V • Perfect Indicative Active 2nd Plural • ★
V • Aorist Indicative Active 2nd Plural • 3

σατε

V • Aorist Indicative Active 2nd Plural • ★
V • Aorist Imperative Active 2nd Plural • ★

▲ ετε

V • Present Indicative Active 2nd Plural • ★ εμι
V • Present Imperative Active 2nd Plural • ★ εμι
V • Imperfect Indicative Active 2nd Plural • ★ εμι
V • 2nd Aorist Indicative Active 2nd Plural • 1 εμι
V • 2nd Aorist Imperative Active 2nd Plural • 1 εμι
V • 2nd Perfect Imperative Active 2nd Plural • 1
V • 2nd Pluperfect Indicative Active 2nd Plural • 1

κετε

V • Perfect Imperative Active 2nd Plural • ★
V • Pluperfect Indicative Active 2nd Plural • ★

σετε

V • Future Indicative Active 2nd Plural • ★

ητε

V • Present Subjunctive Active 2nd Plural • ★ εω αμι εμι υμι 4
V • 2nd Aorist Subjunctive Active 2nd Plural • 1 2 αμι εμι υμι
V • 2nd Aorist Imperative Active 2nd Plural • 2 αμι
V • 2nd Aorist Indicative Active 2nd Plural • 2 αμι
V • Present Indicative Active 2nd Plural • 4
V • Present Imperative Active 2nd Plural • 4
V • Imperfect Indicative Active 2nd Plural • 4
V • Aorist Subjunctive Active 2nd Plural • 3
V • 2nd Aorist Indicative Passive 2nd Plural • 1
V • 2nd Aorist Subjunctive Passive 2nd Plural • 1
V • 2nd Perfect Subjunctive Active 2nd Plural • 1
V • 2nd Aorist Imperative Passive 2nd Plural • 1

θητε

V • Aorist Indicative Passive 2nd Plural • ★
V • Aorist Subjunctive Passive 2nd Plural • ★
V • Aorist Imperative Passive 2nd Plural • ★

αιητε

V • Present Optative Active 2nd Plural • αμι
V • 2nd Aorist Optative Active 2nd Plural • αμι

ειητε

V • Present Optative Active 2nd Plural • εμι
V • 2nd Aorist Optative Active 2nd Plural • εμι
V • 2nd Aorist Optative Passive 2nd Plural • 1

θειητε

V • Aorist Optative Passive 2nd Plural • ★

οιητε

V • Present Optative Active 2nd Plural • εω οω ομι
V • 2nd Aorist Optative Active 2nd Plural • ομι

κητε

V • Perfect Subjunctive Active 2nd Plural • ★

σητε

V • Aorist Subjunctive Active 2nd Plural • ★

ῳητε

V • Present Optative Active 2nd Plural • αω

αιτε

V • Present Optative Active 2nd Plural • αμι
V • 2nd Aorist Optative Active 2nd Plural • αμι 2
V • Aorist Optative Active 2nd Plural • 3

σαιτε

V • Aorist Optative Active 2nd Plural • ★

ειτε

V • Present Indicative Active 2nd Plural • εω
V • Present Imperative Active 2nd Plural • εω
V • Imperfect Indicative Active 2nd Plural • εω
V • Present Optative Active 2nd Plural • εμι
V • Future Indicative Active 2nd Plural • 3
V • 2nd Aorist Optative Active 2nd Plural • εμι
V • 2nd Aorist Optative Passive 2nd Plural • 1
V • 2nd Pluperfect Indicative Active 2nd Plural • 1

θειτε

V • Aorist Optative Passive 2nd Plural • ★

κειτε

V • Pluperfect Indicative Active 2nd Plural • ★

OLTE

V • Present Optative Active 2nd Plural • ★ εω οω ομι υμι
V • 2nd Aorist Optative Active 2nd Plural • 1 2 ομι
V • 2nd Perfect Optative Active 2nd Plural • 1
V • Future Optative Active 2nd Plural • 3

KOLTE

V • Perfect Optative Active 2nd Plural • ★

σOLTE

V • Future Optative Active 2nd Plural • ★

OTE

V • Present Indicative Active 2nd Plural • ομι
V • Present Imperative Active 2nd Plural • ομι
V • Imperfect Indicative Active 2nd Plural • ομι
V • 2nd Aorist Indicative Active 2nd Plural • ομι
V • 2nd Aorist Imperative Active 2nd Plural • ομι

υTE

V • Present Indicative Active 2nd Plural • υμι
V • Present Imperative Active 2nd Plural • υμι
V • Imperfect Indicative Active 2nd Plural • υμι
V • 2nd Aorist Indicative Active 2nd Plural • υμι 2
V • 2nd Aorist Imperative Active 2nd Plural • υμι 2

OυTE

V • Present Indicative Active 2nd Plural • οω
V • Present Imperative Active 2nd Plural • οω
V • Imperfect Indicative Active 2nd Plural • οω

ωTE

V • Present Subjunctive Active 2nd Plural • οω ομι
V • 2nd Aorist Subjunctive Active 2nd Plural • ομι 2
V • 2nd Aorist Indicative Active 2nd Plural • 2
V • 2nd Aorist Imperative Active 2nd Plural • 2

ῳTE

V • Present Optative Active 2nd Plural • αω
V • 2nd Aorist Optative Active 2nd Plural • 2

η

η

V • Present Imperative Active 2nd Singular • αμι 4
V • Imperfect Indicative Active 3rd Singular • αμι εμι 4 5
V • 2nd Aorist Indicative Active 3rd Singular • αμι 2
V • 2nd Aorist Indicative Passive 3rd Singular • 1
V • 2nd Pluperfect Indicative Active 1st Singular • 1
N • See Case Ending List

ῃ

V • Present Indicative Middle/Passive 2nd Singular • ★ εω εμι 4
V • Present Subjunctive Active 3rd Singular • ★ εω αμι εμι υμι 4
V • Present Subjunctive Mid/Pass 2nd Singular • ★ εω αμι εμι υμι 4
V • Present Indicative Active 3rd Singular • 4
V • Future Indicative Middle 2nd Singular • 3
V • Aorist Subjunctive Active 3rd Singular • 3
V • Aorist Subjunctive Middle 2nd Singular • 3
V • 2nd Aorist Subjunctive Active 3rd Singular • αμι εμι υμι 1 2
V • 2nd Aorist Subjunctive Middle 2nd Singular • αμι εμι 1
V • 2nd Aorist Subjunctive Passive 3rd Singular • 1
V • 2nd Perfect Subjunctive Active 3rd Singular • 1
N • See Case Ending List

θη

V • Aorist Indicative Passive 3rd Singular • ★

θῃ

V • Aorist Subjunctive Passive 3rd Singular • ★

αιη

V • Present Optative Active 3rd Singular • αμι
V • 2nd Aorist Optative Active 3rd Singular • αμι 2

ειη

V • Present Optative Active 3rd Singular • εμι
V • 2nd Aorist Optative Active 3rd Singular • εμι
V • 2nd Aorist Optative Passive 3rd Singular • 1

θειη

V • Aorist Optative Passive 3rd Singular • ★

οιη

V • Present Optative Active 3rd Singular • εω οω ομι
V • 2nd Aorist Optative Active 3rd Singular • ομι 2
V • Future Optative Active 3rd Singular • 3
V • 2nd Perfect Optative Active 3rd Singular • 1

κοιη

V • Perfect Optative Active 3rd Singular • ★

κη

V • Pluperfect Indicative Active 1st Singular • ★

κῃ

V • Perfect Subjunctive Active 3rd Singular • ★

μενη

V • See Periphrastic Chart
P • See Participle Chart A

μενῃ

P • See Participle Chart A

ση

V • Future Indicative Middle 2nd Singular • ★
V • Future Perfect Indicative Passive 2nd Singular • ★
V • Aorist Subjunctive Active 3rd Singular • ★
V • Aorist Subjunctive Middle 2nd Singular • ★
P • See Participle Chart B

(θ)ησῃ

V • (1st) 2nd Future Indicative Passive 2nd Singular • ★ 1

ῳη

V • Present Optative Active 3rd Singular • αω

V • 2nd Aorist Optative Active 3rd Singular • ομι 2

ι

ι

N • See Case Ending List

αι

V • Aorist Optative Active 3rd Singular • 3
V • Aorist Imperative Middle 2nd Singular • 3
I • Aorist Active • 3
N • See Case Ending List

*θαι

I • Perfect Middle/Passive • LQ

σθαι

I • Perfect Middle/Passive • ★ D

ασθαι

I • Present Middle/Passive • αω αμι 4
I • 2nd Aorist Middle • αμι
I • Aorist Middle • 3

σασθαι

I • Aorist Middle • ★

εσθαι

I • Present Middle/Passive • ★ εμι
I • 2nd Aorist Middle • εμι 1

σεσθαι

I • Future Middle • ★
I • Future Perfect Passive • ★

(θ)ησεσθαι

I • (1st) 2nd Future Passive • ★ 1

ησθαι

I • Present Middle/Passive • 4

εισθαι

I • Present Middle/Passive • εω
I • Future Middle • 3

οσθαι

I • Present Middle/Passive • ομι
I • 2nd Aorist Middle • ομι

υσθαι

I • Present Middle/Passive • υμι

ουσθαι

I • Present Middle/Passive • οω

φθαι

I • Perfect Middle/Passive • L

χθαι

I • Perfect Middle/Passive • G

(κ)υιαι

V • See Periphrastic Chart
P • (1st) 2nd Perfect Active Nominative Feminine Plural • ★ 1

μαι

V • Perfect Indicative Middle/Passive 1st Singular • ★ C

αμαι

V • Present Indicative Middle/Passive 1st Singular • αμι

εμαι

V • Present Indicative Middle/Passive 1st Singular • εμι

ομαι

V • Present Indicative Middle/Passive 1st Singular • ★ ομι

σομαι

V • Future Indicative Middle 1st Singular • ★
V • Future Perfect Indicative Passive 1st Singular • ★

(θ)ησομαι

V • (1st) 2nd Future Indicative Passive 1st Singular • ★ 1

υμαι

V • Present Indicative Middle/Passive 1st Singular • υμι

ουμαι

V • Present Indicative Middle/Passive 1st Singular • εω οω
V • Future Indicative Middle 1st Singular • 3

ωμαι

V • Present Subjunctive Middle/Passive 1st Singular • ★ V MI 4
V • Present Indicative Middle/Passive 1st Singular • αω 4
V • Aorist Subjunctive Middle 1st Singular • 3
V • 2nd Aorist Subjunctive Middle 1st Singular • αμι εμι ομι 1

σωμαι

V • Aorist Subjunctive Middle 1st Singular • ★

ναι

I • Present Active • 5

αναι

I • Present Active • αμι
I • 2nd Aorist Active • 2

εναι

I • Present Active • εμι
I • 2nd Perfect Active • 1

κεναι

I • Perfect Active • ★

μεναι

V • See Periphrastic Chart
P • See Participle Chart A

ηναι

I • 2nd Aorist Active • αμι 2
I • 2nd Aorist Passive • 1

θηναι
I • Aorist Passive • ★

ειναι
I • 2nd Aorist Active • εμι

οναι
I • Present Active • ομι

υναι
I • Present Active • υμι
I • 2nd Aorist Active • υμι 2

ουναι
I • 2nd Aorist Active • ομι

ωναι
I • 2nd Aorist Active • 2

ξαι
V • Perfect Indicative Middle/Passive 2nd Singular • G

σαι
V • Aorist Optative Active 3rd Singular • ★
V • Aorist Imperative Middle 2nd Singular • ★
V • Perfect Indicative Middle/Passive 2nd Singular • ★ LQ D
I • Aorist Active • ★
P • See Participle Chart B

ασαι
V • Present Indicative Middle/Passive 2nd Singular • αω αμι 4

εσαι
V • Present Indicative Middle/Passive 2nd Singular • εμι

οσαι
V • Present Indicative Middle/Passive 2nd Singular • ομι

υσαι
V • Present Indicative Middle/Passive 2nd Singular • υμι

ται
V • Perfect Indicative Middle/Passive 3rd Singular • ★ C

αται
V • Present Indicative Middle/Passive 3rd Singular • αω αμι 4
V • Present Subjunctive Middle/Passive 3rd Singular • αω

26

∈ται

V • Present Indicative Middle/Passive 3rd Singular • ★ ∈μι

σ∈ται

V • Future Indicative Middle 3rd Singular • ★
V • Future Perfect Indicative Passive 3rd Singular • ★

(θ)ησ∈ται

V • (1st) 2nd Future Indicative Passive 3rd Singular • ★ 1

ηται

V • Present Subjunctive Middle/Passive 3rd Singular • ★ ∈ω αμι ∈μι υμι 4
V • Present Indicative Middle/Passive 3rd Singular • 4
V • Aorist Subjunctive Middle 3rd Singular • 3
V • 2nd Aorist Subjunctive Middle 3rd Singular • αμι ∈μι 1

σηται

V • Aorist Subjunctive Middle 3rd Singular • ★

∈ιται

V • Present Indicative Middle/Passive 3rd Singular • ∈ω
V • Future Indicative Middle 3rd Singular • 3

νται

V • Perfect Indicative Middle/Passive 3rd Plural • ★

ανται

V • Present Indicative Middle/Passive 3rd Plural • αμι

∈νται

V • Present Indicative Middle/Passive 3rd Plural • ∈μι

ονται

V • Present Indicative Middle/Passive 3rd Plural • ★ ομι

σονται

V • Future Indicative Middle 3rd Plural • ★
V • Future Perfect Indicative Passive 3rd Plural • ★

(θ)ησονται

V • (1st) 2nd Future Indicative Passive 3rd Plural • ★ 1

υνται

V • Present Indicative Middle/Passive 3rd Plural • υμι

ουνται

V • Present Indicative Middle/Passive 3rd Plural • εω οω
V • Future Indicative Middle 3rd Plural • 3

ωνται

V • Present Subjunctive Middle/Passive 3rd Plural • ★ V MI 4
V • Present Indicative Middle/Passive 3rd Plural • αω 4
V • Aorist Subjunctive Middle 3rd Plural • 3
V • 2nd Aorist Subjunctive Middle 3rd Plural • αμι εμι ομι 1

σωνται

V • Aorist Subjunctive Middle 3rd Plural • ★

οται

V • Present Indicative Middle/Passive 3rd Singular • ομι

υται

V • Present Indicative Middle/Passive 3rd Singular • υμι

ουται

V • Present Indicative Middle/Passive 3rd Singular • οω

ωται

V • Present Subjunctive Middle/Passive 3rd Singular • οω ομι
V • 2nd Aorist Subjunctive Middle 3rd Singular • ομι

ψαι

V • Perfect Indicative Middle/Passive 2nd Singular • L

ει

V • Present Indicative Active 3rd Singular • ★ εω
V • Present Indicative Middle/Passive 2nd Singular • ★ εω
V • Present Imperative Active 2nd Singular • εω εμι
V • Future Indicative Active 3rd Singular • 3
V • Future Indicative Middle 2nd Singular • 3
V • Imperfect Indicative Active 3rd Singular • εω εμι
V • 2nd Pluperfect Indicative Active 3rd Singular • 1
N • See Case Ending List

κει

V • Pluperfect Indicative Active 3rd Singular • ★

σει

V • Future Indicative Active 3rd Singular • ★
V • Future Indicative Middle 2nd Singular • ★
V • Future Perfect Indicative Passive 2nd Singular • ★

28

(θ)ησει

V • (1st) 2nd Future Indicative Passive 2nd Singular • ★ 1

θι

V • Present Imperative Active 2nd Singular • 5
V • 2nd Perfect Imperative Active 2nd Singular • MI

αθι

V • 2nd Aorist Imperative Active 2nd Singular • 2

ηθι

V • 2nd Aorist Imperative Active 2nd Singular • αμι 2
V • 2nd Aorist Imperative Passive 2nd Singular • 1

υθι

V • 2nd Aorist Imperative Active 2nd Singular • υμι 2

ωθι

V • 2nd Aorist Imperative Active 2nd Singular • 2

μι

V • Present Indicative Active 1st Singular • 5

ημι

V • Present Indicative Active 1st Singular • αμι εμι

αιμι

V • Aorist Optative Active 1st Singular • 3

σαιμι

V • Aorist Optative Active 1st Singular • ★

οιμι

V • Present Optative Active 1st Singular • ★ εω οω υμι
V • Future Optative Active 1st Singular • 3
V • 2nd Aorist Optative Active 1st Singular • 1
V • 2nd Perfect Optative Active 1st Singular • 1

κοιμι

V • Perfect Optative Active 1st Singular • ★

σοιμι

V • Future Optative Active 1st Singular • ★

υμι

V • Present Indicative Active 1st Singular • υμι

ωμι

V • Present Indicative Active 1st Singular • ομι

ωμι

V • Present Optative Active 1st Singular • αω

οι

V • Present Optative Active 3rd Singular • ★ εω οω υμι
V • Present Indicative Active 3rd Singular • οω
V • Present Indicative Middle/Passive 2nd Singular • οω
V • Present Subjunctive Active 3rd Singular • οω ομι
V • Present Subjunctive Middle/Passive 2nd Singular • οω
V • 2nd Aorist Subjunctive Active 3rd Singular • ομι
V • Future Optative Active 3rd Singular • 3
V • 2nd Aorist Optative Active 3rd Singular • 1
V • 2nd Perfect Optative Active 3rd Singular • 1
N • See Case Ending List

κοι

V • Perfect Optative Active 3rd Singular • ★

μενοι

V • See Periphrastic Chart
P • See Participle Chart A

σοι

V • Future Optative Active 3rd Singular • ★

σι

V • 2nd Perfect Indicative Active 3rd Plural • MI
V • Present Indicative Active 3rd Plural • 5
P • See Participle Chart B

ασι

V • Present Indicative Active 3rd Plural • αμι εμι
V • 2nd Perfect Indicative Active 3rd Plural • 1
P • See Participle Chart B

εασι

V • Present Indicative Active 3rd Plural • εμι

ιασι

V • Present Indicative Active 3rd Plural • εμι

κασι

V • Perfect Indicative Active 3rd Plural • ★

οασι

V • Present Indicative Active 3rd Plural • ομι

υασι

V • Present Indicative Active 3rd Plural • υμι

ησι

V • Present Indicative Active 3rd Singular • αμι εμι

(κ)οσι

P • (1st) 2nd Perfect Active Dative Masculine/Neuter Plural • ★ 1

υσι

V • Present Indicative Active 3rd Singular • υμι
P • See Participle Chart B

ουσι

V • Present Indicative Active 3rd Plural • ★ εω οω
V • Future Indicative Active 3rd Plural • 3
P • See Participle Chart B

σουσι

V • Future Indicative Active 3rd Plural • ★
P • See Participle Chart B

ωσι

V • Present Subjunctive Active 3rd Plural • ★ V MI 4
V • Present Indicative Active 3rd Singular • ομι
V • Present Indicative Active 3rd Plural • αω 4
V • Aorist Subjunctive Active 3rd Plural • 3
V • 2nd Aorist Subjunctive Active 3rd Plural • MI οω 1 2
V • 2nd Aorist Subjunctive Passive 3rd Plural • 1
V • 2nd Perfect Subjunctive Active 3rd Plural • 1
P • See Participle Chart B

θωσι

V • Aorist Subjunctive Passive 3rd Plural • ★

κωσι

V • Perfect Subjunctive Active 3rd Plural • ★

σωσι

V • Aorist Subjunctive Active 3rd Plural • ★

τι

V • Present Indicative Active 3rd Singular • 5

ητι

V • 2nd Aorist Imperative Passive 2nd Singular • 1

θητι

V • Aorist Imperative Passive 2nd Singular • ★

ντι

P • See Participle Chart C

(κ)οτι

P • (1st) 2nd Perfect Active Dative Masculine/Neuter Singular • ★ 1

V

ν

N • See case Ending List

▲ αν

V • Aorist Indicative Active 3rd Plural • 3
V • 2nd Aorist Indicative Active 1st Singular • 2
I • Present Active • αω
P • Present Active Nominative/Accusative Neuter Singular • αμι
P • 2nd Aorist Active Nominative/Accusative Neuter Singular • αμι 2
P • Aorist Active Nominative/Accusative Neuter Singular • 3
N • See Case Ending List

ειαν

V • Aorist Optative Active 3rd Plural • 3

σειαν

V • Aorist Optative Active 3rd Plural • ★

(κ)υιαν

P • (1st) 2nd Perfect Active Accusative Feminine Singular • ★ 1

καν

V • Perfect Indicative Active 3rd Plural • ★
V • Aorist Indicative Active 3rd Plural • 3

σαν

V • Aorist Indicative Active 3rd Plural • ★
V • 2nd Pluperfect Indicative Active 3rd Plural • MI
V • Imperfect Indicative Active 3rd Plural • 5
P • Aorist Active Nominative Masculine Singular • ★
P • See Participle Chart B

ασαν

V • Imperfect Indicative Active 3rd Plural • αμι
V • 2nd Aorist Indicative Active 3rd Plural • 2
P • See Participle Chart B

εσαν

V • Imperfect Indicative Active 3rd Plural • εμι
V • 2nd Aorist Indicative Active 3rd Plural • εμι
V • 2nd Pluperfect Indicative Active 3rd Plural • 1

κεσαν

V • Pluperfect Indicative Active 3rd Plural • ★

ησαν

V • 2nd Aorist Indicative Active 3rd Plural • αμι 2
V • 2nd Aorist Indicative Passive 3rd Plural • 1

θησαν

V • Aorist Indicative Passive 3rd Plural • ★

αιησαν

V • Present Optative Active 3rd Plural • αμι
V • 2nd Aorist Optative Active 3rd Plural • αμι

ειησαν

V • Present Optative Active 3rd Plural • εμι
V • 2nd Aorist Optative Active 3rd Plural • εμι
V • 2nd Aorist Optative Passive 3rd Plural • 1

θειησαν

V • Aorist Optative Passive 3rd Plural • ★

οιησαν

V • Present Optative Active 3rd Plural • εω οω ομι
V • 2nd Aorist Optative Active 3rd Plural • ομι

ῳησαν
V • Present Optative Active 3rd Plural • αω

εισαν
V • 2nd Pluperfect Indicative Active 3rd Plural • 1
P • See Participle Chart B

κεισαν
V • Pluperfect Indicative Active 3rd Plural • ★

οσαν
V • Imperfect Indicative Active 3rd Plural • ομι
V • 2nd Aorist Indicative Active 3rd Plural • ομι

υσαν
V • Imperfect Indicative Active 3rd Plural • υμι
V • 2nd Aorist Indicative Active 3rd Plural • υμι 2
P • See Participle Chart B

ωσαν
V • 2nd Aorist Indicative Active 3rd Plural • 2
P • See Participle Chart B

σθωσαν
V • Perfect Imperative Middle/Passive 3rd Plural • ★

ασθωσαν
V • Present Imperative Middle/Passive 3rd Plural • αω αμι 4
V • 2nd Aorist Imperative Middle 3rd Plural • αμι
V • Aorist Imperative Middle 3rd Plural • 3

σασθωσαν
V • Aorist Imperative Middle 3rd Plural • ★

εσθωσαν
V • Present Imperative Middle/Passive 3rd Plural • ★ εμι
V • 2nd Aorist Imperative Middle 3rd Plural • εμι 1

ησθωσαν
V • Present Imperative Middle/Passive 3rd Plural • 4

εισθωσαν
V • Present Imperative Middle/Passive 3rd Plural • εω

οσθωσαν
V • Present Imperative Middle/Passive 3rd Plural • ομι
V • 2nd Aorist Imperative Middle 3rd Plural • ομι

υσθωσαν

V • Present Imperative Middle/Passive 3rd Plural • υμι

ουσθωσαν

V • Present Imperative Middle/Passive 3rd Plural • οω

ατωσαν

V • Present Imperative Active 3rd Plural • αω αμι
V • Aorist Imperative Active 3rd Plural • 3

σατωσαν

V • Aorist Imperative Active 3rd Plural • ★

ετωσαν

V • Present Imperative Active 3rd Plural • ★ εμι
V • 2nd Aorist Imperative Active 3rd Plural • εμι 1

κετωσαν

V • Perfect Imperative Active 3rd Plural • ★

ητωσαν

V • Present Imperative Active 3rd Plural • 4
V • 2nd Aorist Imperative Active 3rd Plural • αμι
V • 2nd Aorist Imperative Passive 3rd Plural • 1

θητωσαν

V • Aorist Imperative Passive 3rd Plural • ★

ειτωσαν

V • Present Imperative Active 3rd Plural • εω

οτωσαν

V • Present Imperative Active 3rd Plural • ομι
V • 2nd Aorist Imperative Active 3rd Plural • ομι

υτωσαν

V • Present Imperative Active 3rd Plural • υμι
V • 2nd Aorist Imperative Active 3rd Plural • υμι 2

ουτωσαν

V • Present Imperative Active 3rd Plural • οω

ωτωσαν

V • 2nd Aorist Imperative Active 3rd Plural • 2

▲ εν

V • Imperfect Indicative Active 3rd Singular • ★
V • Aorist Indicative Active 3rd Singular • 3
V • 2nd Aorist Indicative Active 3rd Singular • 1
V • 2nd Perfect Indicative Active 3rd Singular • 1
P • Present Active Nominative/Accusative Neuter Singular • εμι
P • 2nd Aorist Active Nominative/Accusative Neuter Singular • εμι 1
P • 2nd Aorist Passive Nominative/Accusative Neuter Singular • 1

θεν

P • Aorist Passive Nominative/Accusative Neuter Singular • ★

αιεν

V • Present Optative Active 3rd Plural • αμι
V • 2nd Aorist Optative Active 3rd Plural • αμι 2
V • Aorist Optative Active 3rd Plural • 3

σαιεν

V • Aorist Optative Active 3rd Plural • ★

ειεν

V • Present Optative Active 3rd Plural • εμι
V • 2nd Aorist Optative Active 3rd Plural • εμι
V • Aorist Optative Active 3rd Singular • 3
V • 2nd Aorist Optative Passive 3rd Plural • 1

θειεν

V • Aorist Optative Passive 3rd Plural • ★

σειεν

V • Aorist Optative Active 3rd Singular • ★

οιεν

V • Present Optative Active 3rd Plural • ★ εω οω ομι υμι
V • Future Optative Active 3rd Plural • 3
V • 2nd Aorist Optative Active 3rd Plural • ομι 1 2
V • 2nd Perfect Optative Active 3rd Plural • 1

κοιεν

V • Perfect Optative Active 3rd Plural • ★

σοιεν

V • Future Optative Active 3rd Plural • ★

κεν

V • Perfect Indicative Active 3rd Singular • ★
V • Aorist Indicative Active 3rd Singular • 3

μεν

V • 2nd Perfect Indicative Active 1st Plural • MI
V • 2nd Pluperfect Indicative Active 3rd Singular • MI

▲ αμεν

V • Present Indicative Active 1st Plural • αμι
V • Imperfect Indicative Active 1st Plural • αμι
V • Aorist Indicative Active 1st Plural • 3
V • 2nd Aorist Indicative Active 1st Plural • 2
V • 2nd Perfect Indicative Active 1st Plural • 1

καμεν

V • Perfect Indicative Active 1st Plural • ★
V • Aorist Indicative Active 1st Plural • 3

σαμεν

V • Aorist Indicative Active 1st Plural • ★

εμεν

V • Present Indicative Active 1st Plural • εμι
V • Imperfect Indicative Active 1st Plural • εμι
V • 2nd Aorist Indicative Active 1st Plural • εμι
V • 2nd Pluperfect Indicative Active 1st Plural • 1

κεμεν

V • Pluperfect Indicative Active 1st Plural • ★

ημεν

V • 2nd Aorist Indicative Active 1st Plural • αμι 2
V • 2nd Aorist Indicative Passive 1st Plural • 1

θημεν

V • Aorist Indicative Passive 1st Plural • ★

αιημεν

V • Present Optative Active 1st Plural • αμι
V • 2nd Aorist Optative Active 1st Plural • αμι

ειημεν

V • Present Optative Active 1st Plural • εμι
V • 2nd Aorist Optative Active 1st Plural • εμι
V • 2nd Aorist Optative Passive 1st Plural • 1

θειημεν

V • Aorist Optative Passive 1st Plural • ★

οιημεν

V • Present Optative Active 1st Plural • εω οω ομι
V • 2nd Aorist Optative Active 1st Plural • ομι

ῳημεν

V • Present Optative Active 1st Plural • αω

αιμεν

V • Present Optative Active 1st Plural • αμι
V • 2nd Aorist Optative Active 1st Plural • αμι 2
V • Aorist Optative Active 1st Plural • 3

σαιμεν

V • Aorist Optative Active 1st Plural • ★

ειμεν

V • Present Optative Active 1st Plural • εμι
V • 2nd Aorist Optative Active 1st Plural • εμι
V • 2nd Aorist Optative Passive 1st Plural • 1
V • 2nd Pluperfect Indicative Active 1st Plural • 1

θειμεν

V • Aorist Optative Passive 1st Plural • ★

κειμεν

V • Pluperfect Indicative Active 1st Plural • ★

οιμεν

V • Present Optative Active 1st Plural • ★ εω οω ομι υμι
V • Future Optative Active 1st Plural • 3
V • 2nd Aorist Optative Active 1st Plural • ομι 1 2
V • 2nd Perfect Optative Active 1st Plural • 1

κοιμεν

V • Perfect Optative Active 1st Plural • ★

σοιμεν

V • Future Optative Active 1st Plural • ★

▲ ομεν

V • Present Indicative Active 1st Plural • ★ ομι
V • Imperfect Indicative Active 1st Plural • ★ ομι
V • 2nd Aorist Indicative Active 1st Plural • ομι 1

σομεν

V • Future Indicative Active 1st Plural • ★

υμεν

V • Present Indicative Active 1st Plural • υμι
V • Imperfect Indicative Active 1st Plural • υμι
V • 2nd Aorist Indicative Active 1st Plural • υμι 2

ουμεν

V • Present Indicative Active 1st Plural • εω οω
V • Imperfect Indicative Active 1st Plural • εω οω
V • Future Indicative Active 1st Plural • 3

ωμεν

V • Present Subjunctive Active 1st Plural • ★ V MI 4
V • Present Indicative Active 1st Plural • αω 4
V • Imperfect Indicative Active 1st Plural • αω 4
V • Aorist Subjunctive Active 1st Plural • 3
V • 2nd Aorist Indicative Active 1st Plural • 2
V • 2nd Aorist Subjunctive Active 1st Plural • MI οω 1 2
V • 2nd Aorist Subjunctive Passive 1st Plural • 1
V • 2nd Perfect Subjunctive Active 1st Plural • 1

ῳμεν

V • Present Optative Active 1st Plural • αω
V • 2nd Aorist Optative Active 1st Plural • 2

θωμεν

V • Aorist Subjunctive Passive 1st Plural • ★

κωμεν

V • Perfect Subjunctive Active 1st Plural • ★

σωμεν

V • Aorist Subjunctive Active 1st Plural • ★

σεν

V • Aorist Indicative Active 3rd Singular • ★

ῳεν

V • Present Optative Active 3rd Plural • αω
V • 2nd Aorist Optative Active 3rd Plural • 2

ην

V • Imperfect Indicative Active 1st Singular • αμι εμι
V • 2nd Aorist Indicative Active 1st Singular • αμι 2
V • 2nd Aorist Indicative Passive 1st Singular • 1
I • Present Active • 4
N • See Case Ending List

θην

V • Aorist Indicative Passive 1st Singular • ★
V • See Dual Chart

αιην

V • Present Optative Active 1st Singular • αμι
V • 2nd Aorist Optative Active 1st Singular • αμι 2

ειην

V • Present Optative Active 1st Singular • εμι
V • 2nd Aorist Optative Active 1st Singular • εμι
V • 2nd Aorist Optative Passive 1st Singular • 1

θειην

V • Aorist Optative Passive 1st Singular • ★

οιην

V • Present Optative Active 1st Singular • εω οω ομι
V • 2nd Aorist Optative Active 1st Singular • ομι 2
V • Future Optative Active 1st Singular • 3
V • 2nd Perfect Optative Active 1st Singular • 1

κοιην

V • Perfect Optative Active 1st Singular • ★

μην

V • Pluperfect Indicative Middle/Passive 1st Singular • ★ C

αμην

V • Imperfect Indicative Middle/Passive 1st Singular • αμι
V • 2nd Aorist Indicative Middle 1st Singular • αμι
V • Aorist Indicative Middle 1st Singular • 3

σαμην

V • Aorist Indicative Middle 1st Singular • ★

εμην

V • Imperfect Indicative Middle/Passive 1st Singular • εμι
V • 2nd Aorist Indicative Middle 1st Singular • εμι

41

αιμην

V • Present Optative Middle/Passive 1st Singular • αμι
V • 2nd Aorist Optative Middle 1st Singular • αμι
V • Aorist Optative Middle 1st Singular • 3

σαιμην

V • Aorist Optative Middle 1st Singular • ★

ειμην

V • Present Optative Middle/Passive 1st Singular • εμι
V • 2nd Aorist Optative Middle 1st Singular • εμι

οιμην

V • Present Optative Middle/Passive 1st Singular • ★ εω οω ομι υμι
V • 2nd Aorist Optative Middle 1st Singular • ομι 1
V • Future Optative Middle 1st Singular • 3

σοιμην

V • Future Optative Middle 1st Singular • ★
V • Future Perfect Optative Passive 1st Singular • ★

(θ)ησοιμην

V • (1st) 2nd Future Optative Passive 1st Singular • ★ 1

ομην

V • Imperfect Indicative Middle/Passive 1st Singular • ★ ομι
V • 2nd Aorist Indicative Middle 1st Singular • ομι 1

υμην

V • Imperfect Indicative Middle/Passive 1st Singular • υμι

ουμην

V • Imperfect Indicative Middle/Passive 1st Singular • εω οω

ωμην

V • Imperfect Indicative Middle/Passive 1st Singular • αω 4

ῳμην

V • Present Optative Middle/Passive 1st Singular • αω

μενην

P • See Participle Chart A

την

V • See Dual Chart

ωην

V • Present Optative Active 1st Singular • αω
V • 2nd Aorist Optative Active 1st Singular • ομι 2

ιν

N • See Case Ending List

ειν

V • 2nd Pluperfect Indicative Active 1st Singular • 1
V • 2nd Pluperfect Indicative Active 3rd Singular • 1
I • Present Active • ★ εω
I • Future Active • 3
I • 2nd Aorist Active • 1

κειν

V • Pluperfect Indicative Active 1st Singular • ★
V • Pluperfect Indicative Active 3rd Singular • ★

σειν

I • Future Active • ★

ξιν

N • See Case Ending List

σιν

P • See Participle Chart B
N • See Case Ending List

ασιν

V • Present Indicative Active 3rd Plural • αμι εμι
V • 2nd Perfect Indicative Active 3rd Plural • 1
P • See Participle Chart B

εασιν

V • Present Indicative Active 3rd Plural • εμι

ιασιν

V • Present Indicative Active 3rd Plural • εμι

κασιν

V • Perfect Indicative Active 3rd Plural • ★

οασιν

V • Present Indicative Active 3rd Plural • ομι

υασιν

V • Present Indicative Active 3rd Plural • υμι

ησιν

V • Present Indicative Active 3rd Singular • αμι εμι

(κ)οσιν

P • (1st) 2nd Perfect Active Dative Masculine/Neuter Plural • ★ 1

υσιν

V • Present Indicative Active 3rd Singular • υμι
P • See Participle Chart B

ουσιν

V • Present Indicative Active 3rd Plural • ★ εω οω
V • Future Indicative Active 3rd Plural • 3
P • See Participle Chart B

σουσιν

V • Future Indicative Active 3rd Plural • ★
P • See Participle Chart B

ωσιν

V • Present Subjunctive Active 3rd Plural • ★ V MI 4
V • Present Indicative Active 3rd Singular • ομι
V • Present Indicative Active 3rd Plural • αω 4
V • Aorist Subjunctive Active 3rd Plural • 3
V • 2nd Aorist Subjunctive Active 3rd Plural • MI 1 2
V • 2nd Aorist Subjunctive Passive 3rd Plural • 1
V • 2nd Perfect Subjunctive Active 3rd Plural • 1
P • See Participle Chart B

θωσιν

V • Aorist Subjunctive Passive 3rd Plural • ★

κωσιν

V • Perfect Subjunctive Active 3rd Plural • ★

σωσιν

V • Aorist Subjunctive Active 3rd Plural • ★

ψιν

N • See Case Ending List

▲ ον

V • Imperfect Indicative Active 1st Singular • ★
V • Imperfect Indicative Active 3rd Plural • ★
V • Aorist Imperative Active 2nd Singular • 3
V • 2nd Aorist Indicative Active 1st Singular • 1

(continued)
V • 2nd Aorist Indicative Active 3rd Plural • 1
P • Present Active Nominative/Accusative Neuter Singular • ★ ομι
P • 2nd Aorist Active Nominative/Accusative Neuter Singular • ομι 1 2
N • See Case Ending List

θον

V • See Dual Chart

μενον

V • See Periphrastic Chart
P • See Participle Chart A

σον

V • Aorist Imperative Active 2nd Singular • ★
P • Future Active Nominative/Accusative Neuter Singular • ★

τον

V • See Dual Chart

υν

V • Imperfect Indicative Active 1st Singular • υμι
V • 2nd Aorist Indicative Active 1st Singular • υμι 2
P • Present Active Nominative/Accusative Neuter Singular • υμι
P • 2nd Aorist Active Nominative/Accusative Neuter Singular • υμι 2
N • See Case Ending List

ουν

V • Imperfect Indicative Active 1st Singular • εω οω ομι
V • Imperfect Indicative Active 3rd Plural • εω οω εμι
I • Present Active • οω
P • Present Active Nominative/Accusative Neuter Singular • εω οω
P • Future Active Nominative/Accusative Neuter Singular • 3

ων

V • Imperfect Indicative Active 1st Singular • αω ομι 4
V • Imperfect Indicative Active 3rd Plural • αω 4
V • 2nd Aorist Indicative Active 1st Singular • 2
P • Present Active Nominative Masculine Singular • ★ V
P • Present Active Nominative/Accusative Neuter Singular • αω
P • 2nd Aorist Active Nominative Masculine Singular • 1
P • Future Active Nominative Masculine Singular • 3
N • See Case Ending List

θων

V • See Dual Chart

*θων

V • Perfect Imperative Middle/Passive 3rd Plural • LQ

σθων

V • Perfect Imperative Middle/Passive 3rd Plural • ★ D

ασθων

V • Present Imperative Middle/Passive 3rd Plural • αω αμι
V • 2nd Aorist Imperative Middle 3rd Plural • αμι
V • Aorist Imperative Middle 3rd Plural • 3

σασθων

V • Aorist Imperative Middle 3rd Plural • ★

εσθων

V • Present Imperative Middle/Passive 3rd Plural • ★ εμι
V • 2nd Aorist Imperative Middle 3rd Plural • εμι 1

ησθων

V • Present Imperative Middle/Passive 3rd Plural • 4

εισθων

V • Present Imperative Middle/Passive 3rd Plural • εω

οσθων

V • Present Imperative Middle/Passive 3rd Plural • ομι
V • 2nd Aorist Imperative Middle 3rd Plural • ομι

υσθων

V • Present Imperative Middle/Passive 3rd Plural • υμι

ουσθων

V • Present Imperative Middle/Passive 3rd Plural • οω

φθων

V • Perfect Imperative Middle/Passive 3rd Plural • L

χθων

V • Perfect Imperative Middle/Passive 3rd Plural • G

(κ)υιων

P • (1st) 2nd Perfect Active Genitive Feminine Plural • ★ 1

μενων

P • See Participle Chart A

σων

P • Future Active Nominative Masculine Singular • ★
P • See Participle Chart B

των

V • See Dual Chart

ετων

V • 2nd Perfect Imperative Active 3rd Plural • 1

υτων

V • 2nd Perfect Imperative Active 3rd Plural • MI
P • See Participle Chart C

αυτων

V • Present Imperative Active 3rd Plural • αμι
V • 2nd Aorist Imperative Active 3rd Plural • αμι 2
V • Aorist Imperative Active 3rd Plural • 3
P • See Participle Chart C

σαυτων

V • Aorist Imperative Active 3rd Plural • ★
P • See Participle Chart C

εντων

V • Present Imperative Active 3rd Plural • εμι
V • 2nd Aorist Imperative Active 3rd Plural • εμι
V • 2nd Aorist Imperative Passive 3rd Plural • 1
P • See Participle Chart C

θεντων

V • Aorist Imperative Passive 3rd Plural • ★
P • See Participle Chart C

οντων

V • Present Imperative Active 3rd Plural • ★ ομι
V • 2nd Aorist Imperative Active 3rd Plural • ομι 1 2
V • 2nd Perfect Imperative Active 3rd Plural • 1
P • See Participle Chart C

κοντων

V • Perfect Imperative Active 3rd Plural • ★

υντων

V • Present Imperative Active 3rd Plural • υμι
V • 2nd Aorist Imperative Active 3rd Plural • υμι 2
P • See Participle Chart C

ουντων

V • Present Imperative Active 3rd Plural • εω οω
P • See Participle Chart C

ωντων

V • Present Imperative Active 3rd Plural • αω 4
P • See Participle Chart C

(κ)οτων

P • (1st) 2nd Perfect Active Genitive Masculine/Neuter Plural • ★ 1

O

o

N • See Case Ending List

αιο

V • Present Optative Middle/Passive 2nd Singular • αμι
V • 2nd Aorist Optative Middle 2nd Singular • αμι
V • Aorist Optative Middle 2nd Singular • 3

σαιο

V • Aorist Optative Middle 2nd Singular • ★

ειο

V • Present Optative Middle/Passive 2nd Singular • εμι
V • 2nd Aorist Optative Middle 2nd Singular • εμι

οιο

V • Present Optative Middle/Passive 2nd Singular • ★ εω οω ομι υμι
V • 2nd Aorist Optative Middle 2nd Singular • ομι 1
V • Future Optative Middle 2nd Singular • 3

σοιο

V • Future Optative Middle 2nd Singular • ★
V • Future Perfect Optative Passive 2nd Singular • ★

(θ)ησοιο

V • (1st) 2nd Future Optative Passive 2nd Singular • ★ 1

ξο

V • Pluperfect Indicative Middle/Passive 2nd Singular • G
V • Perfect Imperative Middle/Passive 2nd Singular • G

σο

V • Perfect Imperative Middle/Passive 2nd Singular • ★ D LQ
V • Pluperfect Indicative Middle/Passive 2nd Singular • ★ D LQ

ασο

V • Present Imperative Middle/Passive 2nd Singular • αμι
V • Imperfect Indicative Middle/Passive 2nd Singular • αμι

εσο

V • Present Imperative Middle/Passive 2nd Singular • εμι
V • Imperfect Indicative Middle/Passive 2nd Singular • εμι

οσο

V • Present Imperative Middle/Passive 2nd Singular • ομι
V • Imperfect Indicative Middle/Passive 2nd Singular • ομι

υσο

V • Present Imperative Middle/Passive 2nd Singular • υμι
V • Imperfect Indicative Middle/Passive 2nd Singular • υμι

το

V • Pluperfect Indicative Middle/Passive 3rd Singular • ★ C

ατο

V • Imperfect Indicative Middle/Passive 3rd Singular • αω αμι 4
V • 2nd Aorist Indicative Middle 3rd Singular • αμι
V • Aorist Indicative Middle 3rd Singular • 3

σατο

V • Aorist Indicative Middle 3rd Singular • ★

ετο

V • Imperfect Indicative Middle/Passive 3rd Singular • ★ εμι
V • 2nd Aorist Indicative Middle 3rd Singular • εμι 1

ητο

V • Imperfect Indicative Middle/Passive 3rd Singular • 4

αιτο

V • Present Optative Middle/Passive 3rd Singular • αμι
V • 2nd Aorist Optative Middle 3rd Singular • αμι
V • Aorist Optative Middle 3rd Singular • 3

σαιτο

V • Aorist Optative Middle 3rd Singular • ★

ειτο

V • Present Optative Middle/Passive 3rd Singular • εμι
V • 2nd Aorist Optative Middle 3rd Singular • εμι
V • Imperfect Indicative Middle/Passive 3rd Singular • εω

οιτο

V • Present Optative Middle/Passive 3rd Singular • ★ εω οω ομι υμι
V • 2nd Aorist Optative Middle 3rd Singular • ομι 1
V • Future Optative Middle 3rd Singular • 3

σοιτο

V • Future Optative Middle 3rd Singular • ★
V • Future Perfect Optative Passive 3rd Singular • ★

(θ)ησοιτο

V • (1st) 2nd Future Optative Passive 3rd Singular • ★ 1

ντο

V • Pluperfect Indicative Middle/Passive 3rd Plural • ★

αντο

V • Imperfect Indicative Middle/Passive 3rd Plural • αμι
V • 2nd Aorist Indicative Middle 3rd Plural • αμι
V • Aorist Indicative Middle 3rd Plural • 3

σαντο

V • Aorist Indicative Middle 3rd Plural • ★

εντο

V • Imperfect Indicative Middle/Passive 3rd Plural • εμι
V • 2nd Aorist Indicative Middle 3rd Plural • εμι

αιντο

V • Present Optative Middle/Passive 3rd Plural • αμι
V • 2nd Aorist Optative Middle 3rd Plural • αμι
V • Aorist Optative Middle 3rd Plural • 3

σαιντο

V • Aorist Optative Middle 3rd Plural • ★

ειντο

V • Present Optative Middle/Passive 3rd Plural • εμι
V • 2nd Aorist Optative Middle 3rd Plural • εμι 1

οιντο

V • Present Optative Middle/Passive 3rd Plural • ★ εω οω ομι υμι
V • 2nd Aorist Optative Middle 3rd Plural • ομι 1
V • Future Optative Middle 3rd Plural • 3

σοιντο

V • Future Optative Middle 3rd Plural • ★
V • Future Perfect Optative Passive 3rd Plural • ★

(θ)ησοιντο

V • (1st) 2nd Future Optative Passive 3rd Plural • ★ 1

οντο

V • Imperfect Indicative Middle/Passive 3rd Plural • ★ ομι
V • 2nd Aorist Indicative Middle 3rd Plural • ομι 1

υντο

V • Imperfect Indicative Middle/Passive 3rd Plural • υμι

ουντο

V • Imperfect Indicative Middle/Passive 3rd Plural • εω οω

ωντο

V • Imperfect Indicative Middle/Passive 3rd Plural • αω 4

ῳντο

V • Present Optative Middle/Passive 3rd Plural • αω

οτο

V • Imperfect Indicative Middle/Passive 3rd Singular • ομι
V • 2nd Aorist Indicative Middle 3rd Singular • ομι

υτο

V • Imperfect Indicative Middle/Passive 3rd Singular • υμι

ουτο

V • Imperfect Indicative Middle/Passive 3rd Singular • οω

ῳτο

V • Present Optative Middle/Passive 3rd Singular • αω

ψο

V • Pluperfect Indicative Middle/Passive 2nd Singular • L
V • Perfect Imperative Middle/Passive 2nd Singular • L

ῳο

V • Present Optative Middle/Passive 2nd Singular • αω

ς

ς

N • See Case Ending List

▲ ας

V • Imperfect Indicative Active 2nd Singular • αω
V • Aorist Indicative Active 2nd Singular • 3
V • 2nd Aorist Indicative Active 2nd Singular • 2
V • 2nd Perfect Indicative Active 2nd Singular • 1
P • Present Active Nominative Masculine Singular • αμι
P • 2nd Aorist Active Nominative Masculine Singular • αμι 2
P • Aorist Active Nominative Masculine Singular • 3
N • See Case Ending List

ας

V • Present Indicative Active 2nd Singular • αω
V • Present Subjunctive Active 2nd Singular • αω
V • 2nd Aorist Subjunctive Active 2nd Singular • 2

ειας

V • Aorist Optative Active 2nd Singular • 3

σειας

V • Aorist Optative Active 2nd Singular • ★

(κ)υιας

P • (1st) 2nd Perfect Active Genitive Feminine Singular • ★ 1
P • (1st) 2nd Perfect Active Accusative Feminine Plural • ★ 1

κας

V • Perfect Indicative Active 2nd Singular • ★
V • Aorist Indicative Active 2nd Singular • 3 MI

μενας

P • See Participle Chart A

σας

V • Aorist Indicative Active 2nd Singular • ★
P • Aorist Active Nominative Masculine Singular • ★
P • See Participle Chart B

ντας

P • See Participle Chart C

(κ)οτας

P • (1st) 2nd Perfect Active Accusative Masculine Plural • ★ 1

▲ ες

V • Imperfect Indicative Active 2nd Singular • ★
V • 2nd Aorist Indicative Active 2nd Singular • 1
V • 2nd Aorist Imperative Active 2nd Singular • εμι
N • See Case Ending List

ντες

P • See Participle Chart C

(κ)οτες

V • See Periphrastic Chart
P • (1st) 2nd Perfect Active Nominative Masculine Plural • ★ 1

ης

V • Present Indicative Active 2nd Singular • αμι εμι
V • Imperfect Indicative Active 2nd Singular • αμι εμι 4
V • 2nd Aorist Indicative Active 2nd Singular • αμι 2
V • 2nd Aorist Indicative Passive 2nd Singular • 1
V • 2nd Pluperfect Active Indictive 2nd Singular • 1
N • See Case Ending List

ης

V • Present Subjunctive Active 2nd Singular • ★ εω αμι εμι υμι 4
V • Present Indicative Active 2nd Singular • 4
V • Aorist Subjunctive Active 2nd Singular • 3
V • 2nd Aorist Subjunctive Active 2nd Singular • αμι εμι υμι 1 2
V • 2nd Aorist Subjunctive Passive 2nd Singular • 1
V • 2nd Perfect Subjunctive Active 2nd Singular • 1

θης

V • Aorist Indicative Passive 2nd Singular • ★

θῃς

V • Aorist Subjunctive Passive 2nd Singular • ★

αιης

V • Present Optative Active 2nd Singular • αμι
V • 2nd Aorist Optative Active 2nd Singular • αμι 2

ειης

V • Present Optative Active 2nd Singular • εμι
V • 2nd Aorist Optative Active 2nd Singular • εμι
V • 2nd Aorist Optative Passive 2nd Singular • 1

θειης

V • Aorist Optative Passive 2nd Singular • ★

οιης

V • Present Optative Active 2nd Singular • εω οω ομι
V • 2nd Aorist Optative Active 2nd Singular • ομι 2
V • 2nd Perfect Optative Active 2nd Singular • 1
V • Future Optative Active 2nd Singular • 3

κοιης

V • Perfect Optative Active 2nd Singular • ★

κης

V • Pluperfect Indicative Active 2nd Singular • ★

κῃς

V • Perfect Subjunctive Active 2nd Singular • ★

μενης

P • See Participle Chart A

σης

P • See Participle Chart B

σῃς

V • Aorist Subjunctive Active 2nd Singular • ★

ῳης

V • Present Optative Active 2nd Singular • αω
V • 2nd Aorist Optative Active 2nd Singular • ομι 2

ις

N • See Case Ending List

αις

V • Aorist Optative Active 2nd Singular • 3
N • See Case Ending List

(κ)υιαις

P • (1st) 2nd Perfect Active Dative Feminine Plural • ★ 1

μεναις

P • See Participle Chart A

σαις

V • Aorist Optative Active 2nd Singular • ★
P • See Participle Chart B

εις

V • Present Indicative Active 2nd Singular • ★ εω
V • Imperfect Indicative Active 2nd Singular • εω εμι
V • Future Indicative Active 2nd Singular • 3
V • 2nd Pluperfect Indicative Active 2nd Singular • 1
P • Present Active Nominative Masculine Singular • εμι
P • 2nd Aorist Active Nominative Masculine Singular • εμι
P • 2nd Aorist Passive Nominative Masculine Singular • 1
N • See Case Ending List

θεις

P • Aorist Passive Nominative Masculine Singular • ★

κεις

V • Pluperfect Indicative Active 2nd Singular • ★

σεις

V • Future Indicative Active 2nd Singular • ★

οις

V • Present Optative Active 2nd Singular • ★ εω οω υμι
V • Present Indicative Active 2nd Singular • οω
V • Present Subjunctive Active 2nd Singular • οω ομι
V • 2nd Aorist Optative Active 2nd Singular • 1
V • 2nd Perfect Optative Active 2nd Singular • 1
V • Future Optative Active 2nd Singular • 3
V • 2nd Aorist Subjunctive Active 2nd Singular • ομι
N • See Case Ending List

κοις

V • Perfect Optative Active 2nd Singular • ★

μενοις

P • See Participle Chart A

σοις

V • Future Optative Active 2nd Singular • ★

ος

V • 2nd Aorist Imperative Active 2nd Singular • ομι
V • See Periphrastic Chart
P • 2nd Perfect Active Nominative/Accusative Neuter Singular • 1
N • See Case Ending List

κος

V • See Periphrastic Chart
P • Perfect Active Nominative/Accusative Neuter Singular • ★

μενος

V • See Periphrastic Chart
P • See Participle Chart A

ντος

P • See Participle Chart C

(κ)οτος

P • (1st) 2nd Perfect Active Genitive Masculine/Neuter Singular • ★ 1

υς

V • Present Indicative Active 2nd Singular • υμι
V • Imperfect Indicative Active 2nd Singular • υμι
V • 2nd Aorist Indicative Active 2nd Singular • υμι 2
P • Present Active Nominative Masculine Singular • υμι 2
P • 2nd Aorist Active Nominative Masculine Singular • υμι
N • See Case Ending List

ουϛ

V • Imperfect Indicative Active 2nd Singular • οω ομι
P • Present Active Nominative Masculine Singular • ομι
P • 2nd Aorist Active Nominative Masculine Singular • ομι 2
N • See Case Ending List

μενουϛ

P • See Participle Chart A

ωϛ

V • Present Indicative Active 2nd Singular • ομι
V • Imperfect Indicative Active 2nd Singular • ομι
V • 2nd Aorist Indicative Active 2nd Singular • 2
V • See Periphrastic Chart
P • 2nd Perfect Active Nominative Masculine Singular • 1
N • See Case Ending List

ῳϛ

V • Present Subjunctive Active 2nd Singular • ομι
V • 2nd Aorist Subjunctive Active 2nd Singular • ομι 2
V • Present Optative Active 2nd Singular • αω

κωϛ

V • See Periphrastic Chart
P • Perfect Active Nominative Masculine Singular • ★

U

υ

V • Present Imperative Active 2nd Singular • υμι
V • Imperfect Indicative Active 3rd Singular • υμι
V • 2nd Aorist Indicative Active 3rd Singular • υμι 2
N • See Case Ending List

ου

V • Present Imperative Middle/Passive 2nd Singular • ★ εω οω εμι ομι
V • Imperfect Indicative Middle/Passive 2nd Singular • ★ εω οω εμι ομι
V • Present Imperative Active 2nd Singular • οω ομι
V • Imperfect Indicative Active 3rd Singular • οω ομι
V • 2nd Aorist Indicative Middle 2nd Singular • εμι ομι 1
V • 2nd Aorist Imperative Middle 2nd Singular • εμι ομι 1
N • See Case Ending List

μενου

P • See Participle Chart A

ω

ω

V • Present Indicative Active 1st Singular • ★ V 4
V • Present Subjunctive Active 1st Singular • ★ V MI 4
V • Present Imperative Middle/Passive 2nd Singular • αω αμι 4
V • Imperfect Indicative Middle/Passive 2nd Singular • αω 4
V • Imperfect Indicative Active 3rd Singular • ομι
V • Future Indicative Active 1st Singular • 3
V • Aorist Indicative Middle 2nd Singular • 3
V • Aorist Subjunctive Active 1st Singular • 3
V • 2nd Aorist Subjunctive Active 1st Singular • MI 1 2
V • 2nd Aorist Indicative Active 3rd Singular • 2
V • 2nd Aorist Subjunctive Passive 1st Singular • 1
V • 2nd Perfect Subjunctive Active 1st Singular • 1
V • 2nd Aorist Indicative Middle 2nd Singular • αμι
V • 2nd Aorist Imperative Middle 2nd Singular • αμι

ω̣

V • Present Subjunctive Active 3rd Singular • ομι
V • Present Subjunctive Middle/Passive 2nd Singular • ομι
V • 2nd Aorist Subjunctive Active 3rd Singular • ομι 2
V • 2nd Aorist Subjunctive Middle 2nd Singular • ομι
V • Present Optative Active 3rd Singular • αω
N • See Case Ending List

θω

V • Aorist Subjunctive Passive 1st Singular • ★

*θω

V • Perfect Imperative Middle/Passive 3rd Singular • LQ

σθω

V • Perfect Imperative Middle/Passive 3rd Singular • ★ D

ασθω

V • Present Imperative Middle/Passive 3rd Singular • αω αμι 4
V • 2nd Aorist Imperative Middle 3rd Singular • αμι
V • Aorist Imperative Middle 3rd Singular • 3

σασθω

V • Aorist Imperative Middle 3rd Singular • ★

εσθω

V • Present Imperative Middle/Passive 3rd Singular • ★ εμι
V • 2nd Aorist Imperative Middle 3rd Singular • εμι 1

ησθω

V • Present Imperative Middle/Passive 3rd Singular • 4

εισθω

V • Present Imperative Middle/Passive 3rd Singular • εω

οσθω

V • Present Imperative Middle/Passive 3rd Singular • ομι
V • 2nd Aorist Imperative Middle 3rd Singular • ομι

υσθω

V • Present Imperative Middle/Passive 3rd Singular • υμι

ουσθω

V • Present Imperative Middle/Passive 3rd Singular • οω

φθω

V • Perfect Imperative Middle/Passive 3rd Singular • L

χθω

V • Perfect Imperative Middle/Passive 3rd Singular • G

κω

V • Perfect Subjunctive Active 1st Singular • ★

μενω

P • See Participle Chart A

σω

V • Future Indicative Active 1st Singular • ★
V • Aorist Indicative Middle 2nd Singular • ★
V • Aorist Subjunctive Active 1st Singular • ★

τω

V • 2nd Perfect Imperative Active 3rd Singular • MI

ατω

V • Present Imperative Active 3rd Singular • αω αμι
V • Aorist Imperative Active 3rd Singular • 3
V • 2nd Aorist Imperative Active 3rd Singular • 2

σατω

V • Aorist Imperative Active 3rd Singular • ★

ετω

V • Present Imperative Active 3rd Singular • ★ εμι
V • 2nd Aorist Imperative Active 3rd Singular • εμι 1
V • 2nd Perfect Imperative Active 3rd Singular • 1

κετω

V • Perfect Imperative Active 3rd Singular • ★

ητω

V • Present Imperative Active 3rd Singular • 4
V • 2nd Aorist Imperative Active 3rd Singular • αμι 2
V • 2nd Aorist Imperative Passive 3rd Singular • 1

θητω

V • Aorist Imperative Passive 3rd Singular • ★

ειτω

V • Present Imperative Active 3rd Singular • εω

οτω

V • Present Imperative Active 3rd Singular • ομι
V • 2nd Aorist Imperative Active 3rd Singular • ομι

υτω

V • Present Imperative Active 3rd Singular • υμι
V • 2nd Aorist Imperative Active 3rd Singular • υμι

ΟΥΤΩ

V • Present Imperative Active 3rd Singular • οω

ΩΤΩ

V • 2nd Aorist Imperative Active 3rd Singular • 2

Case Endings for
Nouns, Adjectives and Pronouns

α

1st Nominative/Vocative Singular Feminine
1st Vocative Singular Masculine
1st Nom/Acc/Voc Dual Masculine/Feminine
2nd Nom/Acc/Voc Plural Neuter
3rd Accusative Singular Masculine/Feminine
3rd Nominative/Accusative Singular Neuter
3rd Nom/Acc/Voc Plural Neuter
3rd Nom/Acc/Voc Dual Neuter

ᾳ

1st Dative Singular Feminine/Masculine

μα

3rd Nom/Acc/Voc Singular Neuter

ε

2nd Vocative Singular Masculine/Feminine
3rd Nominative/Accusative/Vocative Dual Masc/Fem/Neuter
Accusative Singular [personal pronoun ending]

η

1st Nominative/Vocative Singular Feminine
3rd Nominative/Accusative/Vocative Plural Neuter
3rd Accusative Singular Masculine/Feminine
3rd Nom/Acc/Voc Dual Masculine

ῃ

1st Dative Singular Feminine/Masculine

ι

3rd Dative Singular Masculine/Feminine/Neuter
3rd Vocative Singular Masculine/Feminine

αι

1st Nominative/Vocative Plural Feminine/Masculine
3rd Dative Singular Neuter

ει

3rd Dative Singular Masculine/Feminine/Neuter
3rd Nom/Acc/Voc Dual Masculine/Feminine/Neuter

ξι
3rd Dative Plural Masculine/Feminine • guttural

οι
2nd Nominative/Vocative Plural Masculine/Feminine

σι
3rd Dative Plural Masculine/Feminine

ψι
3rd Dative Plural Masculine/Feminine • labial

ν
3rd Accusative Singular Masculine/Feminine

αν
1st Accusative Singular Feminine/Masculine
3rd Accusative/Vocative Singular Masculine

ην
1st Accusative Singular Feminine/Masculine
3rd Nominative/Vocative Singular Masculine

αιν
1st Genitive/Dative Dual Feminine/Masculine

ιν
3rd Accusative Singular Masculine/Feminine

ξιν
3rd Dative Plural Masculine/Feminine/Neuter • guttural

οιν
3rd Genitive/Dative Dual Masculine/Feminine

σιν
3rd Dative Plural Masculine/Feminine/Neuter

ψιν
3rd Dative Plural Masculine/Feminine/Neuter • labial

ον
2nd Accusative Singular Masculine/Feminine
2nd Nominative/Accusative/Vocative Singular Neuter
3rd Vocative Singular Masculine

σιν
3rd Dative Plural Masculine/Feminine/Neuter

ουν

2nd Accusative Singular Masculine • εο οο
2nd Nominative/Accusative/Vocative Singular Neuter • εο οε

υν

3rd Accusative Singular Masculine/Feminine

ων

Genitive Plural [for all words]
2nd Accusative Singular Masculine • ως/εως
3rd Nominative/Vocative Singular Masculine/Feminine

ων

3rd Genitive/Dative Dual Neuter

ξ

3rd Nominative/Vocative Singular Masculine/Feminine • guttural

ο

2nd Nom/Acc Singular Neuter [special pronominal ending]

ρ

3rd Nominative/Vocative Singular Masculine
3rd Nom/Acc/Voc Singular Neuter

ς

3rd Nominative Singular Masculine/Feminine

ας

1st Accusative Plural Feminine/Masculine
1st Genitive Singular Feminine
1st Nominative Singular Masculine
3rd Accusative Plural Masculine/Feminine
3rd Nominative Singular Masculine
3rd Nom/Acc/Voc Singular Neuter

ες

3rd Nominative/Vocative Plural Masculine/Feminine/Neuter
3rd Accusative Singular Neuter

ης

1st Genitive Singular Feminine
1st Nominative Singular Masculine
3rd Nominative Singular Feminine
3rd Nominative/Vocative Singular Masculine
3rd Nominative/Vocative Plural Masculine

ιϲ

3rd Nominative Singular Masculine/Feminine
3rd Vocative Singular Feminine

αιϲ

1st Dative Plural Feminine/Masculine

ειϲ

3rd Nominative/Accusative Plural Masculine/Feminine
3rd Nominative/Vocative Plural Masculine

οιϲ

2nd Dative Plural Masculine/Feminine/Neuter

οϲ

2nd Nominative Singular Masculine/Feminine
3rd Genitive Singular Masculine/Feminine/Neuter
3rd Nominative/Accusative Singular Neuter

υϲ

3rd Nominative Singular Masculine/Feminine
3rd Accusative Plural Masculine/Feminine

αυϲ

3rd Nominative Singular Feminine
3rd Accusative Plural Feminine

ουϲ

2nd Accusative Plural Masculine/Feminine
2nd Nominative Singular Masculine • εο οο
3rd Genitive Singular Neuter
3rd Nominative Singular Masculine/Feminine
3rd Accusative Plural Masculine/Feminine

ωϲ

2nd Nominative Singular Masculine • ωϲ/εωϲ
2nd Accusative Plural Masculine • ωϲ/εωϲ
3rd Genitive Singular Masculine/Feminine/Neuter

ῳϲ

2nd Dative Plural Masculine • ωϲ/εωϲ

υ

3rd Nominative/Accusative/Vocative Singular Neuter
3rd Vocative Singular Masculine/Feminine

70

αυ

3rd Vocative Singular Feminine

ευ

3rd Vocative Singular Masculine

ου

1st Genitive Singular Masculine
2nd Genitive Singular Masculine/Feminine/Neuter
2nd Vocative Singular Masculine • εο οο
3rd Vocative Singular Masculine/Feminine

##

3rd Nominative/Vocative Singular Masculine/Feminine • labial

ω

2nd Genitive Singular Masculine • ωϛ/εωϛ
2nd Nom/Acc/Voc Dual Masc/Fem/Neuter

ῳ

2nd Dative Singular Masculine/Feminine/Neuter
2nd Nominative Plural Masculine • ωϛ/εωϛ

The Verb εἰμί

εἶ	Present Indicative Active 2nd Singular
εἶεν	Present Optative Active 3rd Plural
εἴη	Present Optative Active 3rd Singular
εἴημεν	Present Optative Active 1st Plural
εἴην	Present Optative Active 1st Singular
εἴης	Present Optative Active 2nd Singular
εἴησαν	Present Optative Active 3rd Plural
εἴητε	Present Optative Active 2nd Plural
εἶμεν	Present Optative Active 1st Plural
εἰμί	Present Indicative Active 1st Singular
εἶναι	Present Active Infinitive
εἰσί	Present Indicative Active 3rd Plural
εἶτε	Present Optative Active 2nd Plural
ἔσει	Future Indicative Middle 2nd Singular
ἔσεσθαι	Future Middle Infinitive
ἔσεσθε	Future Indicative Middle 2nd Plural
ἔσῃ	Future Indicative Middle 2nd Singular
ἐσμέν	Present Indicative Active 1st Plural
ἐσοίμεθα	Future Optative Middle 1st Plural
ἐσόμεν...	Future Participle [See note below]
ἐσοίμην	Future Optative Middle 1st Singular
ἔσοιντο	Future Optative Middle 3rd Plural
ἔσοιο	Future Optative Middle 2nd Singular
ἔσοισθε	Future Optative Middle 2nd Plural
ἔσοιτο	Future Optative Middle 3rd Singular
ἔσομαι	Future Indicative Middle 1st Singular
ἐσόμεθα	Future Indicative Middle 2st Plural
ἔσονται	Future Indicative Middle 3rd Plural
ἔσται	Future Indicative Middle 3rd Singular
ἐστέ	Present Indicative Active 2nd Plural
ἔστε	Present Imperative Active 2nd Plural
ἐστί(ν)	Present Indicative Active 3rd Singular
ἔστω	Present Imperative Active 3rd Singular

ἔστων	Present Imperative Active 3rd Plural
ἔστωσαν	Present Imperative Active 3rd Plural
ᾖ	Present Subjunctive Active 3rd Singular
ἤ	Imperfect Indicative Active 1st Singular
ἦμεν	Imperfect Indicative Active 1st Plural
ἦν	Imperfect Indicative Active 1st Singular
ἦν	Imperfect Indicative Active 3rd Singular
ᾖς	Present Subjunctive Active 2nd Singular
ἦσαν	Imperfect Indicative Active 3rd Plural
ἦσθα	Imperfect Indicative Active 2nd Singular
ἦστε	Imperfect Indicative Active 2nd Plural
ἦτε	Present Subjunctive Active 2nd Plural
ἦτε	Imperfect Indicative Active 2nd Plural
ἴσθι	Present Imperative Active 2nd Singular
ὄν	P • Present Active Nom/Acc Sing Neuter
ὄντ...	Present Participle [See note below]
ὄντων	Present Imperative Active 3rd Plural
οὖσ...	Present Participle [See note below]
ὦ	Present Subjunctive Active 1st Singular
ὦμεν	Present Subjunctive Active 1st Plural
ὤν	P • Present Active Nominative Sing Masc
ὦσι(ν)	Present Subjunctive Active 3rd Plural

A NOTE ABOUT PARTICIPLES:
- The participles for the verb εἰμί can be determined from the Participle charts.
- For the Present Participles, refer to Chart B for the Feminine forms and to Chart C for the Masculine and Neuter forms. For Chart B, connect the 'ου' entry in column one with any entry in column two. For Chart C, connect the 'o' entry in column one with any entry in column two.
- For the Future Participles, refer to Chart A. Connect the 'σο' entry of column one with any entry from column two.

Instructions
for Participle
Charts

Except for a few participle forms that could be more easily listed in the main index, all participle endings can be determined from the three one-page participle charts following. In all, over one thousand participle forms can be read from these charts.

The method is simple. Each chart is divided into two columns. By combining any entry from column one with any entry from column two, the full participle ending can be determined. The reverse order used in the main lists is continued here.

α	μενα
αμι • Present Mid/Pass	Nom/Acc Neuter Plural
αμι • 2nd Aorist Middle	Nom/Acc Feminine Dual
3 • Aorist Middle	μενη
σα	Nominative Feminine Singular
★ • Aorist Middle	μενῃ
ε	Dative Feminine Singular
εμι • Present Mid/Pass	μεναι
εμι • 2nd Aorist Middle	Nominative Feminine Plural
ο	μενοι
ομι ★ • Present Mid/Pass	Nominative Masculine Plural
ομι ★ • 2nd Aorist Middle	μενην
σο	Accusative Feminine Singular
★ • Future Middle	μεναιν
★ • Future Perfect Passive	Genitive/Dative Feminine Dual
(θ)ησο	μενοιν
1 ★ • (1st) 2nd Future Passive	Genitive/Dative Masc/Neuter Dual
υ	μενον
υμι • Present Mid/Pass	Nom/Acc Neuter Singular
ου	Accusative Masculine Singular
εω οω • Present Mid/Pass	μενων
3 • Future Middle	Genitive Masc/Fem/Neuter Plural
ω	μενας
4 αω • Present Mid/Pass	Accusative Feminine Plural
' [Blank]	μενης
★ • Perfect Mid/Pass	Genitive Feminine Singular
	μεναις
	Dative Feminine Plural
	μενοις
	Dative Masc/Neuter Plural
	μενος
	Nominative Masculine Singular
	μενους
	Accusative Masculine Plural
	μενου
	Genitive Masc/Neuter Singular
	μενω
	Nom/Acc Masc/Neuter Dual
	μενῳ
	Dative Masc/Neuter Singular

Participle Chart B

α
MI • Present Mid/Pass
2 αμι • 2nd Aorist Active
3 • Aorist Active

σα
★ • Aorist Active

ει
εμι • Present Active
εμι • 2nd Aorist Active
1 • 2nd Aorist Passive

θει
★ • Aorist Passive

υ
2 υμι • Present Active

ου
εω οω ★ • Present Active
1 2 ομι • 2nd Aorist Active
3 • Future Active

σου
★ • Future Active

ω
4 αω • Present Active

σα
Nominative Feminine Singular
Nom/Acc Feminine Dual

ση
Dative Feminine Singular

σαι
Nominative Feminine Plural

σι
Dative Masc/Neuter Plural

σαν
Accusative Feminine Singular

σαιν
Genitive/Dative Feminine Dual

σιν
Dative Masc/Neuter Plural

σων
Genitive Feminine Plural

σας
Accusative Feminine Plural

σης
Genitive Feminine Singular

σαις
Dative Feminine Plural

Participle Chart C

α
αμι • Present Active
αμι • 2nd Aorist Active
3 • Aorist Active

σα
★ • Aorist Active

ε
εμι • Present Active
εμι • 2nd Aorist Active
1 • 2nd Aorist Passive

θε
★ • Aorist Passive

ο
★ • Present Active
1 • 2nd Aorist Active

σο
★ • Future Active

υ
υμι • Present Active

ου
εω οω ★ • Present Active
3 • Future Active

ω
4 αω • Present Active

ντα
Nom/Acc Neuter Plural
Accusative Masculine Singular

ντε
Nom/Acc Masc/Neuter Dual

ντι
Dative Masc/Neuter Singular

ντοιν
Genitive/Dative Dual

ντων
Genitive Masc/Neuter Plural

ντας
Accusative Masculine Plural

ντες
Nominative Masculine Plural

ντος
Genitive Masc/Neuter Singular

Dual Chart

The main index does not list the dual forms in full. The dual forms can be determined quite simply, however, by the following method.

STEP ONE: The tense, voice, and mood of any dual form can be determined from the 2nd person plural forms in the main lists. To find the appropriate 2nd person plural form, simply replace the basic dual personal ending with the personal ending of the 2nd person plural as follows:

Replace with τε all dual endings in την, τον, των.
Replace with θε all duals ending in θην, θον, θων.

STEP TWO: To determine whether the ending is a 2nd person dual or a third person dual, use the following chart.

PERSON	DUAL ENDING	TENSE AND MOOD OF VERB (as indicated in the main lists)
Second	τον θον	all moods and tenses
Third	των θων	imperative
	την θην	imperfect indicative aorist indicative pluperfect indicative all optatives
	τον θον	indicatives all subjunctives

EXAMPLE: To parse the dual form **σατων**.

1 - The main lists will have indicated that **των** is a dual ending.

2 - Replace the dual personal ending **των** with the 2nd person plural personal ending **τε**. (**σατων-των=σα; σα+τε=σατε**) The form is now **σατε**. [We have simply followed STEP ONE here.]

3 - Find the new ending **σατε** in the main lists. From this entry, determine the tense, mood, and voice. (This particular form is an Aorist Imperative Active.)

4 - Look on the chart above to determine whether the personal ending is a second or third person dual. (This form is a third person dual. [See STEP TWO above.]

5 - The fully parsed form of a word ending in **σατων** is: Aorist Imperative Active 3rd Dual.

Basic Verb Endings

Active		Mid/Pass
------------singular-----------------		
— [ω]	1	μαι
ς [εις]	2	σαι (η)
— [ει]	3	ται
------------plural------------------		
μεν	1	μεθα
τε	2	σθε
σι, ν	3	νται

SECONDARY

Active		Mid/Pass
------------singular----------------		
ν [ον]	1	μην
ς [ες]	2	σο
— [ε, ει]	3	το
------------plural------------------		
μεν	1	μεθα
τε	2	σθε
ν, σαν	3	ντο

• Secondary endings are used for past tenses in the indicative (i.e., Imperfect, Aorist, and Pluperfect.
• Primary endings appear elsewhere (except in the Imperative, which follows).

IMPERATIVES

Active		Middle
------------singular---------------		
varied	2	τε
τω	3	σθω
------------plural------------------		
τε	2	σθε
ντων	3	σθων
[τωσαν]	3	[σθωσαν]

• Aorist Passives take Active endings (rather than the expected Middle endings).
• If 'ε' occurs before the above endings, the ending is Present.
• If 'σα' occurs before the above endings, the ending is Aorist.

Periphrastic Chart

Frequently the Greek verb is expressed by a participle and a form of the verb εἰμί. This is called the Periphrastic form. In the following chart, the tense of εἰμί, the tense of the participle (of the main verbal idea) and the resulting tense of this combined periphrastic form are given.

Tense of εἰμί	Tense of Participle	Tense of Periphrastic Verb
Present Ind.	Perfect	Perfect Indicative
Subjunctive	Perfect	Perfect Subjunctive
Optative	Perfect	Perfect Optative
Imperative	Perfect	Perfect Imperative
Imperfect	Perfect	Pluperfect Indicative

Less Common Constructions

Present	Present	Present
Imperfect	Present	Imperfect
Future	Present	Future
Future	Perfect	Future Perfect

Dialectic Variations

INSTRUCTIONS:

Dialectic variations are not included in the main lists. Such variations can be determined from the following charts (sometimes with reference to the Attic forms in the main lists).

The following points should be noted:

1 - The first column lists the dialectic forms; the second column lists the parallel Attic forms.

2 - The Attic forms are generally not contracted.

3 - Any form marked ‡ is an 'internal' variation (generally the vowels of vowel contract verbs); all other forms are full endings.

AEOLIC

αισα	ασα	participle ending (Chart B)
οισα	ουσα	participle ending (Chart B)
σθαν	σθην	3rd Dual (secondary Mid/Pass ending)
μαν	μην	1st Singular (secondary Mid/Pass ending)
ταν	την	2nd Dual (secondary Active ending)
ην	ειν	I • Active
αις	ας	participle ending (main lists)
		Most αω, εω, οω verbs take MI endings

DORIC

η	αε	αω ‡ (contraction)
η	αη	αω ‡ (contraction)
σευμαι	σομαι	Future Middle 1st Plural
τι	σι	3rd Singular (primary Active ending)
ντι	νσι	3rd Plural (primary Active ending)
σθαν	σθην	3rd Dual (secondary Mid/Pass ending)
μαν	μην	1st Singular (secondary Mid/Pass ending)
ταν	την	2nd Dual (secondary Active ending)
εν	ειν	I • Active
μεν	ναι	I • Aorist Passive
μες	μεν	1st Plural (primary/secondary Active ending)

POETS

μεσθα	μεθα	1st Plural (primary/secondary Mid/Pass ending)
ν	σαν	3rd Plural (secondary Active) for MI verbs
αν	ησαν	3rd Plural for MI verbs
εν	εσαν	3rd Plural for MI verbs
εω	ησαν	Aorist Indicative Passive 3rd Plural
θε/θο		often added to Present and 2nd Aorist stems ‡

HERODOTUS

εα	η	Pluperfect Active 1st Singular
εε	ει	Pluperfect Active 2nd Singular
αι	σαι	2nd Singular (primary Mid/Pass ending)
εαι	εσαι	2nd Singular
αται	νται	Perfect Middle/Passive 3rd Plural
αται	νται	Present Middle/Passive 3rd Plural • MI
ο	σο	2nd Singular (seconday Mid/Pass ending)
αο	ασο	2nd Singular
εο	αο	αω ‡
ατο	ντο	Pluperfect Middle/Passive 3rd Plural
ατο	ντο	Imperfect Middle/Passive 3rd Plural • MI
εας	νς	Pluperfect Active 2nd Singular
ευ	οο	οω ‡ (no contraction)
ευ	οου	οω ‡ (no contraction)
ευ	εσο	2nd Singular (secondary Mid/Pass ending)
εου	αου	αω ‡ (no contraction)
εω	αω	αω ‡ (no contraction)
		Many MI verbs take εω/οω endings

IONIC

αται	νται	Perfect Middle/Passive 3rd Plural
ατο	ντο	Pluperfect Middle/Passive 3rd Plural
ατο	ντο	Optative Middle/Passive 3rd Plural
ευ	εο	εω ‡ (contraction)
ευ	εου	εω ‡ (contraction)

HOMER

αα	αε	αω ‡ (no contraction)
αα	αη	αω ‡ (no contraction)
αᾳ	αει	αω ‡ (no contraction)
αᾳ	αη	αω ‡ (no contraction)
εα	η	Pluperfect Active 1st Singular

σθα	ς	2nd Singular for MI verbs
ησθα	ης	Subjunctive Active 2nd Singular
οισθα	οις	Active Optative 2nd Singular
ε	η	Subjunctive thematic vowel ‡ (Aorist Active/Middle 2nd Plural)
ε	ει	Pluperfect Active 3rd Singular (rare)
εε	ει	Pluperfect Active 3rd Singular (rare)
κετε	ητε	2nd Aorist Subjunctive Passive 2nd Plural
αι	σαι	2nd Singular (primary Mid/Pass ending)
εαι	εσαι	2nd Singular
ηαι	ησαι	2nd Singular
μεναι	ειν	I • Active
μεναι	ναι	I • Aorist Passive
μεναι	ναι	I • Active • MI
ημεναι	αν	I • Present Active • αω
ημεναι	ειν	I • Present Active • εω
θι	(varied)	Present Imperative 2nd Singular • αμι
ωμι	ω	Subjunctive Active 1st Singular
σι	ς	2nd Singular Primary Active Ending
ησι	η	Subjunctive Active 3rd Singular
μεν	ειν	1 • Active
μεν	ναι	I • Active • MI
ειομεν	ωμεν	2nd Aorist Subjunctive Passive 1st Plural
ον	η	Pluperfect Active 1st Singular (rare)
εον	ων	Imperfect Active 1st Singular • αω
σθον	σθην	3rd Dual (past tenses)
τον	την	3rd Dual (past tenses)
ο	ω	Subjunctive thematic vowel ‡ (Aorist Active/Middle 1st Plural)
ο	σο	2nd Singular (secondary Mid/Pass)
αο	ασο	2nd Singular
εο	εσο	2nd Singular
ωο	αο	αω ‡ (no contraction)
ωο	αω	αω ‡ (no contraction)
εας	ης	Pluperfect Active 2nd Singular
ες	ης	Pluperfect Active 2nd Singular (rare)
ηης	ης	2nd Aorist Subjunctive Passive 2nd Singular
ευ	εσο	2nd Singular (secondary Mid/Pass ending)
ειω	εω	εω
ειω	ω	2nd Aorist Subjunctive Passive 1st Singular
οω	αο	αω ‡ (no contraction)

οω	αω	αω ‡ (no contraction)
οω	οο	οω ‡ (no contraction)
οω	οω	οω ‡ (no contraction)
οῳ	αοι	αω ‡ (no contraction)
οῳ	οοι	οω ‡ (no contraction)
ωω	αο	αω ‡ (no contraction)
ωω	αω	αω ‡ (no contraction)

Many MI verbs take εω/οω endings

Finding the Dictionary Form
of Regular Verbs

Some regular verbs undergo changes in their stem. Generally the changes affect the final vowel or consonant of the stem. The following chart will aid in determining the dictionary form of regular verbs that undergo some change in their stem. Simply follow the steps below.

1   Determine the last letter of the root.
2   Locate that letter in column I.
3   Replace the letter in column I with one of the forms in column II.
4   Check a lexicon until one of the forms in column II matches a lexicon entry.
5   If no entry can be found, a more radical change in the stem has likely occurred. To determine the dictionary form of such a verb, refer to the appendix following: 'Finding the Dictionary Form of Irregular Verbs.'

I	II
α	αζω
β	πω, φω
γ	κω, χω, σσω, νω
ε	εζω
η	αω, εω
ι	ιζω
κ	γω, χω
λ	λλω
μ	βω, πω, φω, νω
ξ	γω, κω, χω, σσω
ο	οζω
π	βω, φω
σ	δω, θω, τω
υ	υζω
φ	βω, πω
χ	γω, κω, σσω
ψ	βω, πω, φω

Finding the Dictionary Form
of Irregular Verbs

The dictionary form of most irregular verbs can be found in the following list. The method is simple.

1   Delete all initial vowels and prefixes from the irregular verb. That will leave a shorter stem, and this stem will begin with a consonant.

2   Find this shorter stem in the following list. These stems are listed in the normal alphabetical order used in any lexicon. The word following the shortened stem is the dictionary form for that irregular verb.

β

βα	-	βάπτω
βη	-	βαίνω
	-	ἠβάσκω
βλα	-	βλάπτω
βλαστ	-	βλαστάνω
βλη	-	βάλλω
βρω	-	βιβρώσκω

γ

γ	-	ἄγνυμι
γαγ	-	ἄγω
γεν	-	γίνομαι
	-	γίγνομαι
γημ	-	γαμέω
γηρ	-	γηράσκω
γνω	-	γινώσκω
	-	γιγνώσκω
γον	-	γίνομαι
	-	γίγνομαι
γρη	-	ἐγείρω

δ

δ	-	οἶδα
δαρ	-	δέρω
δαρθ	-	δαρθάνω
δε	-	δέομαι
δεη	-	δείκνυμι
	-	δέομαι
διδα	-	διδάσκω
δο	-	δίδωμι
δρα	-	διδράσκω
δραμ	-	τρέχω
δυ	-	δύνω
δυνη	-	δύναμαι
δω	-	δίδωμι

ζ

ζευ	-	ζεύγνυμι
ζω	-	ζώννυμι

θ

θα	-	θάπτω
θαν	-	θνήσκω
θει	-	τίθημι
θη	-	τίθημι
θιγ	-	θιγγάνω
	-	ἐθίζω
θνη	-	θνήσκω
θορ	-	θρώσκω
θρα	-	τρέφω
θρε	-	τρέφω

κ

κ	-	ἱκνέομαι
κα	-	καίω
καθαρ	-	καθαίρω
καθεδ	-	καθέζομαι
καθερ	-	καθαρίζω
καλυ	-	καλύπτω
καμ	-	κάμνω
	-	κάμπτω
καυ	-	καίω
κερ	-	κεράννυμι
κερδ	-	κερδαίνω
κηκ	-	ἀκούω
κιχ	-	κιγχάνω
κλα	-	κλέπτω
κλαυ	-	κλαίω
κλε	-	κλέπτω
κλη	-	καλέω
κλι	-	κλίνω
κλο	-	κλέπτω
κμη	-	κάμνω
κο	-	κόπτω
κομι	-	κομίζω
κουσ	-	ἀκούω
κορ	-	κορέννυμι
κρα	-	κεράννυμι
κρεμ	-	κρεμάννυμι
κρι	-	κρίνω
κρυ	-	κρύπτω
κταν	-	κτείνω

κτον	-	κτείνω
κυ	-	κύπτω

λ

λ	-	αἱρέω
	-	ἐλαύνω
	-	ὄλλυμι
λα	-	ἔλαυνω
	-	ἱλάσκομαι
λαβ	-	λαμβάνω
λαθ	-	λανθάνω
λακ	-	λάσκω
λασ	-	ἱλασκομαι
λε	-	ὄλλυμι
λευ	-	ἔρχομαι
λη	-	ἐλαύνω
	-	λαγχάνω
	-	λαμβάνω
	-	λανθάνω
ληλ	-	ἔρχομαι
λημ	-	λαμβάνω
λθ	-	ἔρχομαι
λι	-	ἑλίσσω
	-	λείπω
λισθ	-	ὀλισθάνω
λκυ	-	ἕλκω
λλα	-	ἀλλάσσω
λοι	-	λείπω
λω	-	ἁλίσκομαι
	-	ἀναλίσκω
λωλ	-	ὄλλυμι

μ

μα	-	μάσσω
μαθ	-	μανθάβνω
μαρτ	-	ἁμαρτάνω
μεθυ	-	μεθύσκω
μειν	-	μένω
μι	-	μίγνυμι
μνη	-	μιμνήσκω
μο	-	ὄμνυμι
μορ	-	ὀμόργνυμι
μου	-	ὄμνυμι
μωμο	-	ὄμνυμι

90

μφι	- ἀμφιέννυμι	πονθ	- πάσχω	
		πρα	- πιπράσκω	
	ν	πρη	- πίμπρημι	
		πτ	- πέτομαι	
ν	- αἰνέω		- πίπτω	
ναι	- ὀνίνυμι	πτα	- πετάννυμι	
ναλω	- ἀναλίσκω	πτω	- πίπτω	
ναμ	- ὀνίνημι	πυ	- πυνθάνομαι	
νε	- φέρω	πω	- πίνω	
νευ	- νέω			
νεω	- ἀνοίγνυμι		**ρ**	
	- ἀνοίγω			
νη	- φέρω	ρ	- αἱρέω	
	- ὠνέομαι		- εὑρίσκω	
νηλω	- ἀναλίσκω		- λέγω	
νοι	- ἀνοίγνυμι		- ὄρνυμι	
	- ἀνοίγω	ρα	- ῥαίνω	
νο	- φέρω	ργα	- ἐργάζομαι	
		ρε	- αἱρέω	
	ξ		- εὑρίσκω	
		ρει	- ἐρείδω	
ξ	- ἄγω	ρεσ	- ἀρέσκω	
	- ἄγνυμι	ρευ	- ῥέω	
ξη	- αὐξάνω	ρη	- αἱρέω	
	- αὔξω		- εὑρίσκω	
			- λέγω	
	π		- ῥήγνυμι	
π	- λέγω	ρι	- ῥίπτω	
	- πίνω	ρμο	- ἀρμόττω	
πα	- παύω		- ἀρμόζω	
παθ	- πάσχω	ρπ	- ἁρπάζω	
παι	- τύπτω	ρρα	- ῥήγνυμι	
πατα	- τύπτω		- ῥαίνω	
πεισ	- πείθω	ρρε	- λέγω	
πεσ	- πίπτω	ρρη	- εὑρίσκω	
πετ	- πετάννυμι		- λέγω	
πευ	- πυνθάνομαι		- ῥήγνυμι	
πη	- πήγνυμι	ρρι	- ῥίπτω	
πι	- πίνω	ρρυ	- ὀρύσσω	
πλακ	- πλέκω		- ῥέω	
πλασ	- πλάσσω	ρρω	- ῥήγνυμι	
πλη	- πίμπλημι		- ῥώννυμι	
πο	- πίνω	ρυ	- ὀρύσσω	
ποι	- πείθω		- ῥέω	
πομ	- πέμπω	ρωρ	- ὄρνυμι	
			- ὀρύσσω	

91

σ

σ	-	αἴδω
	-	εἰμί
σβ	-	σβέννυμι
σθ	-	αἰσθάνομαι
	-	ἥδομαι
σκα	-	σκάπτω
σκε	-	σκέπτομαι
σκεδ	-	σκεδάννυμι
σπαρ	-	σπείρω
στα	-	ἵστημι
σταλ	-	στέλλομαι
στερ	-	στερίσκω
στη	-	ἵστημι
στρα	-	στρέφω
στρω	-	στρώννυμι
σφα	-	σφάζω
σφρ	-	ὀσφραίνομαι
σχ	-	ἔχω
σω	-	σῴζω

T

τα	-	θάπτω
	-	τείνω
ταλ	-	τέλλω
τεθ	-	τίθημι
τεκ	-	τίκτω
τεμ	-	τέμνω
τεξ	-	τίκτω
τευ	-	τυγχάνω
τεχ	-	τίκτω
τι	-	τίνω
τμη	-	τέμνω
τοκ	-	τίκτω
τρα	-	τρέπω
	-	τρέφω
τρε	-	τρέπω
τρο	-	τρέπω
	-	τρέφω
τρω	-	τιτρώσκω
τυχ	-	τυγχάνω

φ

φα	-	φημί
	-	φαίνω
φαγ	-	ἐσθίω
φεισ	-	φείδομαι
φη	-	φαίνω
	-	φημί
φθα	-	φθάνω
φθαρ	-	φθείρω
φθη	-	φθάνω
φλ	-	ὀφλισκάνω

χ

χ	-	ἄγω
χαν	-	χαίνω
χην	-	χαίνω
χθ	-	ἀπεχθάνομαι
χθε	-	ἄχθομαι
χρη	-	κίχρημι
	-	χράομαι
χυ	-	χέω

ψ

ψευ	-	ψεύδομαι

Also published by The Edwin Mellen Press:

NEW TESTAMENT GREEK
An Introductory Grammar

Watson E. Mills

* Extra-large format (7x10).
* Indexed by paragraph number (not page).
* Complete paradigms distinguish form and functions.
* Two glossaries: Greek to English/English to Greek.
* Option for accent instruction.

ISBN 0-88946-201-1

READING THE NEW TESTAMENT
Exercises for Beginning Readers
of the Greek New Testament

by John Mason and John Hurtgen

"...an excellent student aid to be used in conjunction with my **NEW TESTAMENT GREEK: An Introductory Grammar.** John Mason and John Hurtgen have done a superb job in the preparation of this [teaching] tool."

Watson E. Mills